Criminal Justice (Scotland) Act 1980

CHAPTER 62

ARRANGEMENT OF SECTIONS

PART I

POLICE POWERS

PART II

PROCEDURE AND EVIDENCE

Procedure

ELIZABETH II

Criminal Justice (Scotland) Act 1980

1980 CHAPTER 62

An Act to make further provision as regards criminal justice in Scotland; and for connected purposes.
[13th November 1980]

BE IT ENACTED by the Queen's most Excellent Majesty, by and with the advice and consent of the Lords Spiritual and Temporal, and Commons, in this present Parliament assembled, and by the authority of the same, as follows:—

PART I

POLICE POWERS

Suspect or potential witness may be required by constable to identify himself.

1.—(1) Where a constable has reasonable grounds for suspecting that a person has committed or is committing an offence at any place, he may require—

(*a*) that person, if the constable finds him at that place or at any place where the constable is entitled to be, to give his name and address and may ask him for an explanation of the circumstances which have given rise to the constable's suspicion;

(*b*) any other person whom the constable finds at that place or at any place where the constable is entitled to be and who the constable believes has information relating to the offence, to give his name and address.

(2) The constable may require the person mentioned in paragraph (*a*) of subsection (1) above to remain with him while he (either or both)—

(*a*) verifies any name and address given by the person:

Provided that the constable shall exercise his power

PART I

under this paragraph only where it appears to him that such verification can be obtained quickly;

(*b*) notes any explanation proffered by the person.

(3) A constable may use reasonable force to ensure that the person mentioned in paragraph (*a*) of subsection (1) above remains with him.

(4) A constable shall inform a person, when making a requirement of that person under—

(*a*) paragraph (*a*) of subsection (1) above, of his suspicion and of the general nature of the offence which he suspects that the person has committed or is committing;

(*b*) paragraph (*b*) of subsection (1) above, of his suspicion, of the general nature of the offence which he suspects has been or is being committed and that the reason for the requirement is that he believes the person has information relating to the offence;

(*c*) subsection (2) above, of why the person is being required to remain with him;

(*d*) either of the said subsections, that failure to comply with the requirement may constitute an offence.

(5) A person mentioned in—

(*a*) paragraph (*a*) of subsection (1) above who having been required—

(i) under that subsection to give his name and address; or

(ii) under subsection (2) above to remain with a constable,

fails, without reasonable excuse, to do so, shall be guilty of an offence and liable on summary conviction to a fine not exceeding £200;

(*b*) paragraph (*b*) of the said subsection (1) who having been required under that subsection to give his name and address fails, without reasonable excuse, to do so shall be guilty of an offence and liable on summary conviction to a fine not exceeding £50.

(6) A constable may arrest without warrant any person who he has reasonable grounds for suspecting has committed an offence under subsection (5) above.

Detention and questioning at police station.

2.—(1) Where a constable has reasonable grounds for suspecting that a person has committed or is committing an offence punishable by imprisonment, the constable may, for the purpose of facilitating the carrying out of investigations—

(*a*) into the offence; and

PART I

(b) as to whether criminal proceedings should be instigated against the person,

detain that person and take him as quickly as is reasonably practicable to a police station or other premises and, subject to the following provisions of this section, the detention may continue there.

(2) Detention under subsection (1) above shall be terminated not more than six hours after it begins or (if earlier)—

(a) when the person is arrested ; or

(b) where there are no longer such grounds as are mentioned in the said subsection (1) ;

and when a person has been detained under subsection (1) above for a period of six hours, he shall be informed immediately upon expiry of this period that his detention has been terminated.

(3) Where a person has been released at the termination of a period of detention under subsection (1) above he shall not thereafter be detained, under that subsection, on the same grounds or on any grounds arising out of the same circumstances.

(4) At the time when a constable detains a person under subsection (1) above, he shall inform the person of his suspicion, of the general nature of the offence which he suspects has been or is being committed and of the reason for the detention ; and there shall be recorded—

(a) the place where detention begins and the police station or other premises to which the person is taken ;

(b) the general nature of the suspected offence ;

(c) the time when detention under subsection (1) above begins and the time of the person's arrival at the police station or other premises ;

(d) the time when the person is informed of his rights in terms of subsection (7) below and of subsection (1)(b) of section 3 of this Act and the identity of the constable so informing him ;

(e) where the person requests such intimation to be sent as is specified in section 3(1)(b) of this Act, the time when such request is—

(i) made ;

(ii) complied with ; and

(f) the time of the person's departure from the police station or other premises or, where instead of being released he is arrested in respect of the alleged offence, the time of such arrest.

PART I

(5) Where a person is detained under subsection (1) above, a constable may—

(*a*) put questions to him in relation to the suspected offence:

Provided that this paragraph shall be without prejudice to any existing rule of law as regards the admissibility in evidence of any answer given;

(*b*) exercise the same powers of search as are available following an arrest; and

(*c*) take fingerprints, palmprints and such other prints and impressions as the constable may, having regard to the circumstances of the suspected offence, reasonably consider appropriate:

Provided that the record of the prints and impressions so taken shall be destroyed immediately following a decision not to institute criminal proceedings against the person or on the conclusion of such proceedings otherwise than with a conviction or an order under section 182 or 383 (absolute discharge) or 183(1) or 384(1) (probation) of the 1975 Act.

(6) A constable may use reasonable force in exercising any power conferred by subsection (1), or by paragraph (*b*) or (*c*) of subsection (5), above.

(7) A person detained under subsection (1) above shall be under no obligation to answer any question other than to give his name and address, and a constable shall so inform him both on so detaining him and on arrival at the police station or other premises.

Right to have someone informed when arrested or detained.

3.—(1) Without prejudice to section 19 or 305 of the 1975 Act (intimation to solicitor following arrest), a person who, not being a person in respect of whose custody or detention subsection (3) below applies—

(*a*) has been arrested and is in custody in a police station or other premises, shall be entitled to have intimation of his custody and of the place where he is being held sent, to a person reasonably named by him;

(*b*) is being detained under section 2 of this Act in a police station or other premises, shall be entitled to have intimation of his detention and of the place where he is being detained sent, to a solicitor and to one other person reasonably named by him,

without delay or, where some delay is necessary in the interest of the investigation or the prevention of crime or the apprehension of offenders, with no more delay than is so necessary; and the person shall be informed of such entitlement—

(i) on arrival at the police station or other premises; or

(ii) where he is not arrested, or as the case may be detained, until after such arrival, on such arrest or detention.

(2) Where the person mentioned in paragraph (*a*) of subsection (1) above requests such intimation to be sent as is specified in that paragraph there shall be recorded the time when such request is—

(i) made;

(ii) complied with.

(3) Without prejudice to the said section 19 or 305, a constable shall, where a person who has been arrested and is in such custody as is mentioned in paragraph (*a*) of subsection (1) above or who is being detained as is mentioned in paragraph (*b*) of that subsection appears to him to be a child, send without delay such intimation as is mentioned in the said paragraph (*a*), or as the case may be paragraph (*b*), to that person's parent if known; and the parent—

(*a*) in a case where there is reasonable cause to suspect that he has been involvel in the alleged offence in respect of which the person has been arrested or detained, may; and

(*b*) in any other case shall,

be permitted access to the person.

(4) The nature and extent of any access permitted under subsection (3) above shall be subject to any restriction essential for the furtherance of the investigation or the well-being of the person.

(5) In subsection (3) above—

(*a*) "child" means a person under 16 years of age; and

(*b*) "parent" includes guardian.

Search for offensive weapons.

1953 c. 14.

4.—(1) Where a constable has reasonable grounds for suspecting that any person is carrying an offensive weapon and has committed or is committing an offence under section 1 of the Prevention of Crime Act 1953 (prohibition of carrying of offensive weapons in public) the constable may search that person without warrant, and detain him for such time as is reasonably required to permit the search to be carried out; and he shall inform the person of the reason for such detention.

PART I

(2) Any person who—

(*a*) intentionally obstructs a constable in the exercise of the constable's powers under subsection (1) above; or

(*b*) conceals from a constable acting in the exercise of the said powers an offensive weapon,

shall be guilty of an offence and liable on summary conviction to a fine not exceeding £200.

(3) A constable may arrest without warrant any person who he has reason to believe has committed an offence under subsection (2) above.

(4) In this section, " offensive weapon " has the same meaning as in the said section 1.

Constable may take drunken person to designated place.

5.—(1) Where a constable has power to arrest a person without a warrant for any offence and the constable has reasonable grounds for suspecting that that person is drunk, the constable may, if he thinks fit, take him to any place designated by the Secretary of State for the purposes of this section as a place suitable for the care of drunken persons.

(2) A person shall not by virtue of this section be liable to be detained in any such place as is mentioned in subsection (1) above, but the exercise in his case of the power conferred by this section shall not preclude his being charged with any offence.

PART II

PROCEDURE AND EVIDENCE

Procedure

Judicial examination.

6.—(1) In section 20 of the 1975 Act (accused at examination need not emit a declaration)—

(*a*) in subsection (1), after the words " declaration, and " there shall be inserted the words " subject to section 20A of this Act ";

(*b*) at the end of subsection (3) there shall be added the words " ; and that declaration shall be taken in further examination." ; and

(*c*) after subsection (3) there shall be inserted the following subsections—

" (3A) An accused person may, where subsequent to examination (or further examination) on any charge the prosecutor desires to question him as

PART II

regards an extrajudicial confession (whether or not a full admission) allegedly made by him, to or in the hearing of an officer of police, which is relevant to the charge and as regards which he has not previously been examined, be brought before the sheriff for further examination.

(3B) Where the accused is brought before the sheriff for further examination it shall be in the power of the sheriff to delay that examination for a period not exceeding 24 hours in order to allow time for the attendance of the accused's solicitor.

(3C) Any proceedings before the sheriff in examination or further examination shall be conducted in chambers and outwith the presence of any co-accused.".

(2) After section 20 of the 1975 Act there shall be inserted the following sections—

" Accused at examination may be questioned by prosecutor.

20A.—(1) Subject to the following provisions of this section, an accused on being brought before the sheriff for examination on any charge (whether that examination is the first examination or a further examination) may be questioned by the prosecutor in so far as such questioning is directed towards eliciting any denial, explanation, justification or comment which the accused may have as regards—

(*a*) matters averred in the charge:

Provided that the particular aims of a line of questions under this paragraph shall be to determine—

(i) whether any account which the accused can give ostensibly discloses a category of defence (as for example alibi, incrimination, or the consent of an alleged victim); and

(ii) the nature and particulars of that defence;

(*b*) the alleged making by the accused, to or in the hearing of an officer of police, of an extrajudicial confession (whether or not a full admission) relevant to the charge:

Provided that questions under this paragraph may only be put if the accused has, before the examination, received from the prosecutor or from an officer of police a written record of the confession allegedly made; or

PART II

(c) what is said in any declaration emitted in regard to the charge by the accused at the examination.

(2) The prosecutor shall, in framing questions in exercise of his power under subsection (1) above, have regard to the following principles—

(a) the questions should not be designed to challenge the truth of anything said by the accused;

(b) there should be no reiteration of a question which the accused has refused to answer at the examination; and

(c) there should be no leading questions;

and the sheriff shall ensure that all questions are fairly put to, and understood by, the accused.

(3) The accused, where he is represented by a solicitor at the judicial examination, shall be told by the sheriff that he may consult that solicitor before answering any question.

(4) With the permission of the sheriff, the solicitor for the accused may ask the accused any question the purpose of which is to clarify any ambiguity in an answer given by the accused to the prosecutor at the examination or to give the accused an opportunity to answer any question which he has previously refused to answer.

(5) An accused may decline to answer a question under subsection (1) above; and, where he is subsequently tried on the charge mentioned in that subsection or on any other charge arising out of the circumstances which gave rise to the charge so mentioned, his having so declined may be commented upon by the prosecutor, the judge presiding at the trial, or any co-accused, only where and in so far as the accused (or any witness called on his behalf) in evidence avers something which could have been stated appropriately in answer to that question.

(6) The procedure in relation to examination under this section shall be prescribed by Act of Adjournal under this Act.

Record to be made of proceedings at examination.

20B—(1) The prosecutor shall provide for a *verbatim* record to be made by a shorthand writer of all questions to and answers and declarations by, the accused in examination, or further examination, under sections 20 and 20A of this Act.

(2) The shorthand writer shall sign the transcript of the notes taken by him and shall certify that it is a complete and accurate record of the said questions, answers and declarations; and, subject to subsection (4) below, it shall for all purposes be so deemed.

(3) Subject to subsections (5) and (6) below, within 14 days of the date of examination or further examination, the prosecutor shall—

(a) serve a copy of the transcript on the accused examined; and

(b) serve a further such copy on the solicitor (if any) for that accused.

(4) Subject to subsections (5) and (6) below, where notwithstanding the certification mentioned in subsection (2) above the said accused or the prosecutor is of the opinion that a transcript served under paragraph (a) of subsection (3) above contains an error or is incomplete he may—

(a) within 10 days of service under the said paragraph (a), serve notice of such opinion on the prosecutor or as the case may be the said accused; and

(b) within 14 days of service under paragraph (a) of this subsection, apply to the sheriff for the error or incompleteness to be rectified;

and the sheriff shall within seven days of the application hear the prosecutor and the said accused in chambers and may authorise rectification:

Provided that where—

(i) the person on whom notice is served under paragraph (a) of this subsection agrees with the opinion to which that notice relates the sheriff may dispense with such hearing;

(ii) the said accused neither attends, nor secures that he is represented at, such hearing it shall, subject to paragraph (i) above, nevertheless proceed.

(5) Where at the time of a further examination a trial diet is already fixed and the interval between the further examination and that diet is not sufficient to allow of the time limits specified in subsections (3) and (4) above, the sheriff shall (either or both)—

(a) direct that those subsections shall apply in the case with such modifications as to time limits as he shall specify;

PART II

(*b*) postpone the trial diet:

Provided that postponement under paragraph (*b*) above alone shall only be competent where the sheriff considers that to proceed under paragraph (*a*) above alone, or paragraphs (*a*) and (*b*) above together, would not be practicable.

(6) Any time limit mentioned in subsections (3) and (4) above (including any such time limit as modified by a direction under subsection (5) above) may be extended, in respect of the case, by the High Court.

(7) In so far as it is reasonably practicable so to arrange, the sheriff who deals with any application made under subsection (4) above shall be the sheriff before whom the examination (or further examination) to which the application relates was conducted.

(8) Any decision of the sheriff, as regards rectification under subsection (4) above, shall be final.

(9) A copy of—

(*a*) a transcript required by paragraph (*a*) of subsection (3) above to be served on an accused or by paragraph (*b*) of that subsection to be served on his solicitor ; or

(*b*) a notice required by paragraph (*a*) of subsection (4) above to be served on an accused or on the prosecutor,

may either be personally served on the accused, solicitor or prosecutor (as the case may be) or sent to him by registered post or by the recorded delivery service ; and a written execution purporting to be signed by the person who served such transcript or notice, together with, where appropriate, a post office receipt for the relative registered or recorded delivery letter shall be sufficient evidence of service of such a copy.".

(3) For section 151 of the 1975 Act (accused's declaration in solemn proceedings to be received in evidence without being sworn to by witnesses), there shall be substituted the following section—

" Record of proceedings at examination to be received in evidence without being sworn to by witnesses.

151.—(1) Subject to subsection (2) below, the record made, under section 20B of this Act (with any rectification, authorised under subsection (4) of that section, incorporated), of proceedings at the examination of an accused shall be received in evidence without being sworn to by witnesses, and it shall not be necessary to insert the names of any witnesses to the record in any list of witnesses, either for the prosecution or for the defence.

PART II

(2) Subject to sections 20B(2) and 76(1)(*b*) of this Act, on the application of either an accused or the prosecutor, the court may refuse to allow the record or some part of the record to be read to the jury; and at the hearing of such application it shall be competent for the defence to adduce as witnesses the persons who were present during the proceedings mentioned in subsection (1) above and for the defence and for the prosecutor to examine those witnesses upon any matters regarding the said proceedings.

(3) " Record " in subsection (2) above comprises, as regards any trial, each record included, under section 78(2) of this Act, in the list of productions.".

(4) For section 352 of the 1975 Act (accused's declaration, in summary proceedings, to be received in evidence without being sworn to by witnesses), there shall be sustituted the following section—

" Record of proceedings at examination to be received in evidence without being sworn to by witnesses.

352.—(1) Subject to subsection (2) below, the record made, under section 20B of this Act (with any rectification, authorised under subsection (4) of that section, incorporated), of proceedings at the examination of an accused shall be received in evidence without being sworn to by witnesses.

(2) Subject to section 20B(2) of this Act and to subsection (4) below, on the application of either an accused or the prosecutor, the court may refuse to admit the record or some part of the record as evidence; and at the hearing of such application it shall be competent for the defence to adduce as witnesses the persons who were present during the proceedings mentioned in subsection (1) above and for the defence and for the prosecutor to examine those witnesses upon any matters regarding the said proceedings.

(3) " Record " in subsection (2) above comprises, as regards any trial, each record which it is sought to have received in evidence under subsection (1) above.

(4) Except on cause shown, an application under subsection (2) above shall not be heard unless notice of at least 10 clear days has been given to the court and to the other parties.".

Jurisdiction of district courts.

7.—(1) Except in so far as any enactment (including this Act or an enactment passed after this Act) otherwise provides, the statutory offences which it shall be competent for a district

PART II

court to try shall be those in respect of which the maximum penalty which may be imposed does not exceed 60 days imprisonment or a fine of £200 or both.

1972 c. 20.

(2) Nothing in subsection (1) above shall empower a district court to try an offence specified in Schedule 4 to the Road Traffic Act 1972 in respect of which disqualification from driving or endorsement of a driving licence is either obligatory or discretionary following conviction.

(3) Without prejudice to section 289D of the 1975 Act (power to alter sums specified in certain provisions) it shall be competent, whether or not the accused has been previously convicted of an offence inferring dishonest appropriation of property, for any of the following offences to be tried in the district court—

theft or reset of theft, falsehood, fraud or wilful imposition, breach of trust or embezzlement where (in any such case) the amount concerned does not exceed £200;

and accordingly in section 285 of the 1975 Act (certain crimes not to be tried in inferior courts)—

(i) in paragraph (*b*) (iii) for the words "£25" there shall be substituted the words "£200"; and

(ii) in paragraph (*b*), sub-paragraph (iv) and the proviso shall cease to have effect.

Trial on indictment of summary offences.

8.—(1) Any offence which may under the provisions of any enactment (including this Act or an enactment passed after this Act) be tried only summarily, being an offence which, if it had been triable on indictment, could competently have been libelled as an additional or alternative charge in the indictment, may (the provisions of this or any other enactment notwithstanding) be libelled in an indictment and may be tried accordingly.

(2) A person shall not be liable to any higher penalty on conviction on indictment of an offence to which subsection (1) above applies than he would have been on summary conviction.

Citation of defence witness for precognition.

9.—(1) The sheriff may, on the application of an accused, grant warrant to cite any person (other than a co-accused), who is alleged to be a witness in relation to any offence of which the accused has been charged, to appear before the sheriff in chambers at such time or place as shall be specified in the citation, for precognition on oath by the accused or his solicitor in relation to that offence, if the court is satisfied that it is reasonable to require such precognition on oath in the circumstances.

(2) Any person who, having been duly cited to attend for precognition under subsection (1) above and having been given at least 48 hours notice, fails without reasonable excuse to attend

shall be guilty of an offence and shall be liable on summary conviction to a fine not exceeding £50 or to imprisonment for a period not exceeding 21 days; and the court may issue a warrant for the apprehension of the person concerned, ordering him to be brought before a sheriff for precognition on oath. PART II

(3) Any person who, having been duly cited to attend for precognition under subsection (1) above, attends but—

(i) refuses to give information within his knowledge or to produce evidence in his possession; or

(ii) prevaricates in his evidence,

shall be guilty of an offence and shall be liable to be summarily subjected forthwith to a fine not exceeding £50 or to imprisonment for a period not exceeding 21 days.

Identification parades.

10.—(1) Subject to subsection (2) below, the sheriff may, on an application by an accused at any time after the accused has been charged with an offence, order that, in relation to the alleged offence, the prosecutor shall hold an identification parade in which the accused shall be one of those constituting the parade.

(2) The sheriff shall make an order in accordance with subsection (1) above only after giving the prosecutor an opportunity to be heard and only if—

(*a*) an identification parade, such as is mentioned in subsection (1) above, has not been held at the instance of the prosecutor;

(*b*) after a request by the accused, the prosecutor has refused to hold, or has unreasonably delayed holding, such an identification parade; and

(*c*) the sheriff considers the application under subsection (1) above to be reasonable.

(3) An application under subsection (1) above shall be by petition.

(4) For the purpose of allowing legal aid to be given in relation to identification parades the Legal Aid (Scotland) Act 1967 shall be amended as follows— 1967 c. 43.

(*a*) in section 1 of that Act (scope and general conditions of legal aid—

(i) in subsection (2), after the word " which " there shall be inserted the words " (or, in the case of the legal aid mentioned in subsection (5)(*b*) below, in contemplation of which) ";

PART II

(ii) for subsection (5) there shall be substituted the following subsection—

"(5) Legal aid shall consist of representation, on the terms provided for by this Act—

(*a*) by a solicitor and so far as necessary by counsel (including all such assistance, other than that mentioned in paragraph (*b*) below, as is usually given by solicitor or counsel in the steps preliminary or incidental to any proceedings or in arriving at or giving effect to a settlement to prevent or bring to an end any proceedings);

(*b*) by a solicitor at any identification parade held, by or on behalf of the prosecutor, in connection with or in contemplation of criminal proceedings against the person so represented.

In this subsection "prosecutor" has the same meaning as in Part III of the Criminal Procedure (Scotland) Act 1975."; and

(iii) in subsection (7), after sub-paragraph (ii) there shall be inserted the following words—

"or

(iii) the legal aid is that mentioned in subsection (5)(*b*) of this section;";

(*b*) in section 2 of that Act (financial conditions of legal aid)—

(i) in subsection (5), after the words "legal aid" where they first occur, there shall be inserted the words ", other than that mentioned in section 1(5)(*b*) of this Act,"; and

(ii) after subsection (5) there shall be inserted the following subsection—

"(5AA) Notwithstanding the provisions of subsection (2) of this section, the legal aid mentioned in section 1(5)(*b*) of this Act shall be available to a person without inquiry into his resources.";

(*c*) in section 6 of that Act (entitlement to select solicitor or counsel) at the end of subsection (1) there shall be inserted the following proviso—

": Provided that, where in pursuance of arrangements made by the Law Society in accordance with any scheme for the time being in force under section

PART II

8 of this Act a solicitor is available for the special purpose of giving the legal aid mentioned in section 1(5)(*b*) of this Act, this subsection shall not apply in relation to that legal aid." ; and

(*d*) in section 16 of that Act (rules of court), in subsection (2), after the words " in connection with " where they first occur, there shall be inserted the words " (or, in the case of the legal aid mentioned in section 1(5)(*b*) of this Act, in contemplation of) ".

Discharge and assignation of diets in summary procedure.

11. In section 314 of the 1975 Act (orders of court on complaint)—

(*a*) in subsection (2), after the word " subsection " there shall be inserted the words—

" of a judge—

(*a*) to pronounce an order of court assigning a diet for the disposal of the case may be exercised on his behalf by the clerk of court ;

(*b*) " ;

(*b*) in subsection (3) the words " or a later " shall cease to have effect ;

(*c*) at the end there shall be added the following subsections—

" (4) Where the prosecutor and the accused make joint application to the court (orally or in writing) for postponement of a diet which has been fixed, the court shall discharge the diet and fix in lieu thereof a later diet unless the court considers that it should not do so because there has been unnecessary delay on the part of one or more of the parties.

(5) Where the prosecutor has intimated to the accused that he desires to postpone or accelerate a diet which has been fixed, and the accused refuses, or any of the accused refuse, to make a joint application to the court for that purpose, the prosecutor may make an incidental application for that purpose under section 310 of this Act ; and, after giving the parties an opportunity to be heard, the court may discharge the diet and fix in lieu thereof a later diet or, as the case may be, an earlier diet.

(6) Where an accused has intimated to the prosecutor and to all the other accused that he desires such postponement or acceleration and the prosecutor refuses, or any of the other accused refuse, to make a joint application to the court for that purpose, the

PART II

accused who has so intimated may apply to the court for that purpose; and, after giving the parties an opportunity to be heard, the court may discharge the diet and fix in lieu thereof a later diet or, as the case may be, an earlier diet.".

Abolition of mandatory first diet in solemn procedure.

12. It shall no longer be mandatory to fix two diets of appearance in every case in solemn proceedings; and accordingly the 1975 Act shall have effect subject to the amendments contained in Schedule 4 to this Act.

Written notice of evidence incriminating co-accused in solemn procedure.

13. In section 82 of the 1975 Act (written notice of special defence etc.), for subsection (1) there shall be substituted the following subsection—

"(1) It shall not be competent for an accused to state a special defence or to lead evidence calculated to exculpate the accused by incriminating a co-accused unless—

(*a*) a plea of special defence, or as the case may be, notice of intention to lead such evidence, has been lodged not less than 10 clear days before the trial diet; or

(*b*) the accused having satisfied the court that there was good reason for paragraph (*a*) above not being complied with, such plea or notice has been lodged before the oath is administered to the jury.".

Prevention of delay in trials.

14.—(1) For section 101 of the 1975 Act there shall be substituted the following section—

"Prevention of delay in trials.

101.—(1) An accused shall not be tried on indictment for any offence unless such trial is commenced within a period of 12 months of the first appearance of that accused on petition in respect of that offence; and, failing such commencement within that period, the accused shall be discharged forthwith and thereafter he shall be for ever free from all question or process for that offence:

Provided that—

(i) nothing in this subsection shall bar the trial of an accused for whose arrest a warrant has been granted for failure to appear at a diet in the case;

(ii) on application made for the purpose, the sheriff or, where an indictment has been served on the accused in respect of the High Court, a single judge of that court, may on cause shown extend the said period of 12 months.

(2) Subject to subsections (3), (4) and (5) below, an accused who is committed for any offence until liberated in due course of law shall not be detained by virtue of that committal for a total period of more than—

(*a*) 80 days, unless within that period the indictment is served on him, which failing he shall be liberated forthwith; or

(*b*) 110 days, unless the trial of the case is commenced within that period, which failing he shall be liberated forthwith and thereafter he shall be for ever free from all question or process for that offence.

(3) A single judge of the High Court may, on application made to him for the purpose, for any sufficient cause extend the period mentioned in subsection (2)(*a*) above:

Provided that he shall not extend the said period if he is satisfied that, but for some fault on the part of the prosecution, the indictment could have been served within that period.

(4) A single judge of the High Court may, on application made to him for the purpose, extend the period mentioned in subsection (2)(*b*) above where he is satisfied that delay in the commencement of the trial is due to—

(*a*) the illness of the accused or of a judge;

(*b*) the absence or illness of any necessary witness; or

(*c*) any other sufficient cause which is not attributable to any fault on the part of the prosecutor.

(5) The grant or refusal of any application to extend the periods mentioned in this section may be appealed against by note of appeal presented to the High Court; and that Court may affirm, reverse or amend the determination made on such application.

(6) For the purposes of this section, a trial shall be taken to commence when the oath is administered to the jury.".

(2) After section 331 of the 1975 Act there shall be inserted the following section—

"Prevention of delay in trials.

331A.—(1) Subject to subsections (2) and (3) below, a person charged with a summary offence shall not be detained in that respect for a total of more

PART II

than forty days after the bringing of the complaint in court unless his trial is commenced within that period, failing which he shall be liberated forthwith and thereafter he shall be for ever free from all question or process for that offence.

(2) The sheriff may, on application made to him for the purpose, extend the period mentioned in subsection (1) above and order the accused to be detained awaiting trial for such period as he thinks fit where he is satisfied that delay in the commencement of the trial is due to—

(*a*) the illness of the accused or of a judge ;

(*b*) the absence or illness of any necessary witness ; or

(*c*) any other sufficient cause which is not attributable to any fault on the part of the prosecutor.

(3) The grant or refusal of any application to extend the period mentioned in subsection (1) above may be appealed against by note of appeal presented to the High Court ; and that Court may affirm, reverse or amend the determination made on such application.

(4) For the purposes of this section, a trial shall be taken to commence when the first witness is sworn.".

Intermediate diet in summary procedure.

15. After section 337 of the 1975 Act there shall be added the following section—

"Intermediate diet.

337A.—(1) The court may, at any time, as respects a case which is adjourned for trial, fix a diet (to be known as an intermediate diet) for the purpose of ascertaining—

(*a*) the state of preparation of the prosecutor and of the accused with respect to their cases ; and

(*b*) whether the accused intends to adhere to the plea of not guilty.

(2) At an intermediate diet, the court may ask the prosecutor and the accused any question for the purposes mentioned in subsection (1) above.

(3) The accused shall attend an intermediate diet of which he has received intimation or to which he has been cited.

PART II

(4) A plea of guilty may be tendered at the intermediate diet; and section 336 of this Act shall apply accordingly.".

Procedure where accused desires to plead guilty under solemn procedure.

16. For section 102 of the 1975 Act there shall be substituted the following section—

"Procedure where accused desires to plead guilty.

102.—(1) Where an accused intimates in writing to the Crown Agent that he intends to plead guilty and desires to have his case disposed of at once, the accused may be served with an indictment (unless one has already been served) and a notice to appear at a diet of the appropriate court not less than four clear days after the date of the notice; and it shall not be necessary to lodge or give notice of any list of witnesses or productions.

(2) In subsection (1) above, "appropriate court" means—

(*a*) in a case where at the time of the intimation mentioned in that subsection an indictment had not been served, either the High Court or the sheriff court; and

(*b*) in any other case, the court specified in the notice served under section 75 of this Act on the accused.

(3) If at any such diet the accused pleads not guilty to the charge or pleads guilty only to a part of the charge, and the prosecutor declines to accept such restricted plea, the diet shall be deserted *pro loco et tempore,* and thereafter the cause may proceed in accordance with the other provisions of this Part of this Act except that in a case mentioned in paragraph (*b*) of subsection (2) above the court may postpone the trial diet and the period of such postponement shall not count towards any time limit applying in respect of the case.".

Failure of accused to attend diet in summary procedure.

17. In section 338 of the 1975 Act (failure of accused to appear) the existing words shall be subsection (1) of that section and after that subsection there shall be inserted the following subsections—

"(2) An accused who without reasonable excuse fails to attend any diet of which he has been given due notice, shall be guilty of an offence and liable on summary conviction—

(*a*) to a fine not exceeding £200; and

PART II

(*b*) to a period of imprisonment not exceeding—

(i) in the district court, 60 days; or

(ii) in the sheriff court, 3 months.

(3) The penalties provided for in subsection (2) above may be imposed in addition to any other penalty which it is competent for the court to impose, notwithstanding that the total of penalties imposed may exceed the maximum penalty which it is competent to impose in respect of the original offence.

(4) An accused may be dealt with for an offence under subsection (2) above either at his diet of trial for the original offence or at a separate diet.".

Desertion of trial diet.

18.—(1) In section 127 of the 1975 Act (procedure where trial does not take place) after subsection (1) there shall be inserted the following subsection—

" (1A) The prosecutor shall not raise a fresh libel in a case where the court has deserted the trial diet *simpliciter* (and its decision in that regard has not been reversed on appeal).".

(2) After section 338 of the said Act there shall be added the following section—

"Desertion of trial diet.

338A.—(1) It shall be competent at the diet of trial, at any time before the first witness is sworn, for the court, on the application of the prosecutor, to desert the diet *pro loco et tempore*.

(2) If, at a diet of trial, the court refuses an application by the prosecutor to adjourn the trial or to desert the diet *pro loco et tempore*, and the prosecutor is unable or unwilling to proceed with the trial, the court shall desert the diet *simpliciter*.

(3) Where the court has deserted a diet *simpliciter* under subsection (2) above (and the court's decision in that regard has not been reversed on appeal), it shall not be competent for the prosecutor to raise a fresh libel.".

No case to answer.

19.—(1) After section 140 of the 1975 Act there shall be inserted the following section—

"No case to answer.

140A.—(1) Immediately after the close of the evidence for the prosecution, the accused may intimate to the court his desire to make a submission that he has no case to answer both—

(*a*) on an offence charged in the indictment; and

(*b*) on any other offence of which he could be convicted under the indictment were the offence charged the only offence so charged.

(2) Such a submission shall be heard by the judge in the absence of the jury.

(3) If, after hearing both parties, the judge is satisfied that the evidence led by the prosecution is insufficient in law to justify the accused being convicted of the offence charged in respect of which the submission has been made or of such other offence as is mentioned, in relation to that offence, in paragraph (*b*) of subsection (1) above, he shall acquit him of the offence charged in respect of which the submission has been made and the trial shall proceed only in respect of any other offence charged in the indictment.

(4) If, after hearing both parties, the judge is not satisfied as is mentioned in subsection (3) above, he shall reject the submission and the trial shall proceed, with the accused entitled to give evidence and call witnesses, as if such submission had not been made.".

(2) After section 345 of the 1975 Act there shall be inserted the following section—

"No case to answer.

345A.—(1) Immediately after the close of the evidence for the prosecution, the accused may intimate to the court his desire to make a submission that he has no case to answer both—

(*a*) on an offence charged in the complaint; and

(*b*) on any other offence of which he could be convicted under the complaint were the offence charged the only offence so charged.

(2) If, after hearing both parties, the court is satisfied that the evidence led by the prosecution is insufficient in law to justify the accused being convicted of the offence charged in respect of which the submission has been made or of such other offence as is mentioned, in relation to that offence, in paragraph (*b*) of subsection (1) above, it shall acquit him of the offence charged in respect of which the submission has been made, and the trial shall proceed only in respect of any other offence charged in the complaint.

(3) If, after hearing both parties, the court is not satisfied as is mentioned in subsection (2) above,

PART II

it shall reject the submission and the trial shall proceed, with the accused entitled to give evidence and call witnesses, as if such submission had not been made.".

Correction of entries.

20. After section 227 of the 1975 Act there shall be inserted the following provision—

"Correction of entries.

227A.—(1) Subject to the provisions of this section, it shall be competent to correct an entry in—

(*a*) the record of proceedings in a solemn prosecution ; or

(*b*) the extract of a sentence passed or an order of court made in such proceedings,

in so far as that entry constitutes an error of recording or is incomplete.

(2) Such entry may be corrected—

(*a*) by the clerk of the court, at any time before either the sentence (or order) of the court is executed or, on appeal, the proceedings are transmitted to the Clerk of Justiciary ;

(*b*) by the clerk of the court, under the authority of the court which passed the sentence or made the order, at any time after the execution of the sentence (or order) of the court but before such transmission as is mentioned in paragraph (*a*) above ; or

(*c*) by the clerk of the court under the authority of the High Court in the case of a remit under subsection (4)(*b*) below.

(3) A correction in accordance with paragraph (*b*) or (*c*) of subsection (2) above shall be intimated to the prosecutor and to the former accused or his solicitor.

(4) Where, during the course of an appeal, the High Court becomes aware of an erroneous or incomplete entry, such as is mentioned in subsection (1) above, the court—

(*a*) may consider and determine the appeal as if such entry were corrected ; and

(*b*) either before or after the determination of the appeal, may remit the proceedings to the court of first instance for correction in accordance with subsection (2)(*c*) above.

(5) Any correction under subsections (1) and (2) above by the clerk of the court shall be authenticated

PART II

by his signature and, if such correction is authorised by a court, shall record the name of the judge or judges authorising such correction and the date of such authority." ;

and the same provision shall (with the appropriate section number) be substituted for section 439 of the 1975 Act, except that, in paragraph (*a*) of subsection (1) of the provision, for the word " solemn " there shall be substituted the word " summary ".

Trial may proceed in accused's absence if he misconducts himself.

21. In section 145(1) of the 1975 Act (trial in open court), at the end there shall be added the following proviso—

" : Provided that, if during the course of his trial an accused so misconducts himself that in the view of the court a proper trial cannot take place unless he is removed, the court may order him to be removed for so long as his conduct may make necessary and the trial to proceed in his absence; but if he is not legally represented the court shall appoint counsel or a solicitor to represent his interests during such absence.".

Restrictions on report of proceedings involving person under 16.

22. For section 169 of the 1975 Act there shall be substituted the following provision—

"Restrictions on report of proceedings involving person under 16.

169.—(1) No newspaper report of any proceedings in a court shall reveal the name, address or school, or include any particulars calculated to lead to the identification, of any person under the age of 16 years concerned in the proceedings, either—

(*a*) as being a person against or in respect of whom the proceedings are taken; or

(*b*) as being a witness therein;

nor shall any picture which is, or includes, a picture of a person under the age of 16 years so concerned in the proceedings be published in any newspaper in a context relevant to the proceedings:

Provided that, in any case—

(i) where the person is concerned in the proceedings as a witness only and no one against whom the proceedings are taken is under the age of 16 years, the foregoing provisions of this subsection shall not apply unless the court so directs;

(ii) the court may at any stage of the proceedings if satisfied that it is in the public interest so to do, direct that the requirements of this section (including such requirements as applied by a direction under paragraph (i) above) shall be dispensed with to such extent as the court may specify;

PART II

(iii) the Secretary of State may, after completion of the proceedings, if so satisfied by order dispense with the said requirements to such extent as may be specified in the order.

(2) This section shall, with the necessary modifications, apply in relation to sound and television broadcasts as it applies in relation to newspapers.

(3) A person who publishes matter in contravention of this section shall be guilty of an offence and liable on summary conviction to a fine not exceeding £500.

(4) In this section, references to a court shall not include a court in England, Wales or Northern Ireland." ;

and the same provision shall (with the appropriate section number) be substituted for section 374 of the 1975 Act.

Peremptory challenge of jurors.

23. The number of peremptory challenges allowed to each accused, and to the prosecutor, as respects the jurors in any trial shall be reduced from five to three ; and accordingly for subsection (1) of section 130 of the 1975 Act (challenges and objections to jurors) there shall be substituted the following subsection:

"(1) In any trial each accused may challenge three jurors, as may the prosecutor, without giving any reason.".

Seclusion of jury after retiral.

24.—(1) In section 153 of the 1975 Act (seclusion of jury after retiral)—

(*a*) in subsection (2), after the word "and" there shall be inserted the words ", except in so far as is provided for, or is made necessary, by an instruction under subsection (3A) below," ; and

(*b*) for subsection (3) there shall be substituted the following subsections—

"(3) Except in so far as is provided for, or is made necessary, by an instruction under subsection (3A) below, until the jury intimate that they are ready to return their verdict—

(*a*) no person shall visit the jury and no person (save the judge—

(i) in giving a direction, whether or not sought under paragraph (*b*) below ; or

PART II

(ii) in response to a request made under that paragraph),

shall communicate with them:

Provided that the judge may, for the purposes of this subsection, authorise a person to act on his behalf; and

(*b*) no juror shall come out of the jury room other than to receive or seek a direction from the judge or to make a request—

(i) for an instruction under subsection (3A) (*a*), (*c*) or (*d*) below; or

(ii) regarding any matter in the cause (as, for example, to have made available for examination by them any production).

(3A) The judge may give such instructions as he considers appropriate as regards—

(*a*) the provision of meals and refreshments for the jury;

(*b*) the making of arrangements for overnight accommodation for the jury and for their continued seclusion if such accommodation is provided;

(*c*) the communication of a personal or business message, unconnected with any matter in the cause, from a juror to another person (or *vice versa*); or

(*d*) the provision of medical treatment, or other assistance, immediately required by a juror.".

(2) In section 154 of the 1975 Act (oral verdicts), the words from "; and provided also" to the end shall cease to have effect.

Interpretation of 1975 Act.

25. In section 462(1) of the 1975 Act (interpretation)—

(*a*) for the definition of "officer of law" there shall be substituted the following definition—

"" officer of law " includes, in relation to the service and execution of any warrant, citation, petition, indictment, complaint, list of witnesses, order, notice, or other proceeding or document—

(i) any macer, messenger-at-arms, sheriff officer or other person having authority to execute a warrant of the court;

(ii) any constable within the meaning of the Police (Scotland) Act 1967; 1967 c. 77.

PART II

(iii) where the person upon whom service or execution is effected is in prison at the time of service on him, any prison officer; and

(iv) any person (or class of persons) authorised in that regard for the time being by the Lord Advocate or by the Secretary of State;";

(*b*) for the definition of "probationer" there shall be substituted the following definition—

"" probationer" means a person who is under supervision by virtue of a probation order or who was under such supervision at the time of the commission of any relevant offence or failure to comply with such order;".

Evidence

Routine evidence.

26.—(1) For the purposes of any proceedings for an offence under any of the enactments specified in column 1 of Schedule 1 to this Act, a certificate purporting to be signed by a person or persons specified in column 2 thereof, and certifying the matter specified in column 3 thereof shall, subject to subsection (3) below, be sufficient evidence of that matter and of the qualification or authority of that person or those persons.

(2) For the purposes of any summary criminal proceedings, a report purporting to be signed by two authorised forensic scientists shall, subject to subsection (3) below, be sufficient evidence of any fact (or conclusion as to fact) contained in the report and of the authority of the signatories.

In the foregoing provisions of this subsection, "authorised" means authorised by the Secretary of State to make a report to which this subsection shall apply.

(3) Subsections (1) and (2) above shall not apply to a certificate, or as the case may be report, tendered on behalf of the prosecution—

(*a*) unless a copy has been served on the accused not less than fourteen days before his trial; or

(*b*) where the accused, not less than six days before his trial, or by such later time before his trial as the court may in special circumstances allow, has served notice on the prosecutor that the accused challenges the matter, qualification or authority mentioned in subsection (1) above or as the case may be the fact, conclusion or authority mentioned in subsection (2) above.

(4) A copy of a certificate, or as the case may be report, required by subsection (3) above, or of a conviction or extract

PART II

conviction required by subsection (8) below, to be served on the accused or of a notice required by either of those subsections or by subsection (6) or (7) below to be served on the prosecutor may either be personally served on the accused or the prosecutor (as the case may be) or sent to him by registered post or by the recorded delivery service; and a written execution purporting to be signed by the person who served such certificate or notice, together with, where appropriate, a post office receipt for the relative registered or recorded delivery letter shall be sufficient evidence of service of such a copy.

(5) At any trial of an offence under summary procedure it shall be presumed that the person who appears in answer to the complaint is the person charged by the police with the offence unless the contrary is alleged.

(6) Where in a trial an autopsy report is lodged as a production by the prosecutor it shall be presumed that the body of the person identified in that report is the body of the deceased identified in the indictment or complaint, unless the accused not less than six days before the trial, or by such later time before the trial as the court may in special circumstances allow, gives notice that the contrary is alleged.

(7) At the time of lodging an autopsy or forensic science report as a production the prosecutor may intimate to the accused that it is intended that only one of the pathologists or forensic scientists (whom the prosecutor shall specify) purporting to have signed the report shall be called to give evidence in respect thereof; and the evidence of that pathologist or forensic scientist shall be sufficient evidence of any fact (or conclusion as to fact) contained in the report and of the qualifications of the signatories, unless the accused, not less than six days before the trial, or by such later time before the trial as the court may in special circumstances allow, serves notice on the prosecutor that he requires the attendance at the trial of the other pathologist or forensic scientist also.

(8) In any proceedings for an offence under section 99 (*b*) of the Road Traffic Act 1972 (driving while disqualified) a conviction or an extract conviction— 1972 c. 20.

(i) of which a copy has been served on the accused not less than fourteen days before his trial;

(ii) which purports to be signed by the clerk of court; and

(iii) which shows that the person named therein is disqualified for holding or obtaining a driving licence,

PART II

shall be sufficient evidence of the application of that disqualification to the accused, unless, not less than six days before his trial, he serves notice on the prosecutor that he denies such application.

Parties may examine each other's witnesses etc.

27. After section 82 of the 1975 Act there shall be inserted the following section—

"Parties may examine each other's witnesses etc.

82A. It shall be competent for the prosecutor to examine any witness or put in evidence any production included in any list or notice lodged by the accused, and it shall be competent for an accused to examine any witness or put in evidence any production included in any list or notice lodged by the prosecutor or by a co-accused.".

Co-accused competent witness for defence.

28. In each of sections 141 and 346 of the 1975 Act (accused and spouse competent witnesses for defence)—

(*a*) in paragraph (*a*) of the proviso, at the end there shall be added the words—

" or in accordance with subsection (2) or (3) below ";

(*b*) the provisions of the section as so amended shall be subsection (1) of the section; and

(*c*) after that subsection there shall be added the following subsections—

" (2) The accused may—

(*a*) with the consent of a co-accused, call that other accused as a witness on the accused's behalf; or

(*b*) ask a co-accused any question in cross-examination if that co-accused gives evidence,

but he may not do both in relation to the same co-accused.

(3) The prosecutor or the accused may call as a witness a co-accused who has pleaded guilty to all charges against him which remain before the court (whether or not he has been sentenced); and the party calling such co-accused as a witness shall not require to give notice thereof, but the court may grant any other party such adjournment or postponement of the trial as may seem just.".

PART II

Spouse to be competent witness.

29. For each of sections 143 and 348 of the 1975 Act there shall be substituted the following section (with the appropriate section number)—

"Spouse to be competent witness.

(1) The spouse of a person charged with an offence may be called as a witness—

(*a*) by that person;

(*b*) by a co-accused or by the prosecutor without the consent of that person.

(2) Nothing in this section shall—

(*a*) make the spouse of an accused a compellable witness for a co-accused or for the prosecutor in a case where such spouse would not be so compellable at common law;

(*b*) compel a spouse to disclose any communication made between the spouses during the marriage.

(3) The failure of the spouse of an accused to give evidence shall not be commented on by the defence or the prosecutor.".

Additional evidence and evidence in replication.

30.—(1) For section 149 of the 1975 Act (witness may be recalled) there shall be substituted the following sections—

" Additional evidence.

149.—(1) The judge may, on a motion of the prosecutor or defence made after the close of that party's evidence and before the commencement of the speeches to the jury, permit him to lead additional evidence; but such permission shall only be granted where the judge—

(*a*) considers that the additional evidence is *prima facie* material; and

(*b*) accepts that at the time the party's evidence was closed either—

(i) the additional evidence was not available and could not reasonably have been made available; or

(ii) the materiality of such additional evidence could not reasonably have been foreseen by the party.

(2) The judge may permit the additional evidence to be led notwithstanding that—

(*a*) a witness or production concerned is not included in any list lodged by the parties

PART II

and that the notice required by sections 81 and 82(2) of this Act has not been given; or

(*b*) a witness must be recalled.

(3) The judge may, when granting a motion in terms of this section, adjourn or postpone the trial before permitting the additional evidence to be led.

Evidence in replication.

149A.—(1) The judge may, on a motion of the prosecutor made after the close of the defence evidence and before the commencement of the speeches to the jury, permit the prosecutor to lead additional evidence for the purpose of—

(*a*) contradicting evidence, led by the defence, which could not reasonably have been anticipated by the prosecutor; or

(*b*) providing such proof as is mentioned in section 147 of this Act.

(2) The judge may permit the additional evidence to be led notwithstanding that—

(*a*) a witness or production concerned is not included in any list lodged by the parties and that the notice required by sections 81 and 82(2) of this Act has not been given; or

(*b*) a witness must be recalled.

(3) The judge may when granting a motion in terms of this section, adjourn or postpone the trial before permitting the additional evidence to be led.".

(2) For section 350 of the 1975 Act (witness may be recalled) there shall be substituted the following sections—

"Additional evidence.

350.—(1) The judge may, on a motion of the prosecutor or defence made after the close of that party's evidence and before the prosecutor proceeds to address the judge on the evidence, permit that party to lead additional evidence; but such permission shall only be granted where the judge—

(*a*) considers that the additional evidence is *prima facie* material; and

(*b*) accepts that at the time the party's evidence was closed either—

(i) the additional evidence was not available and could not reasonably have been made available; or

PART II

(ii) the materiality of such additional evidence could not reasonably have been foreseen by the party.

(2) The judge may permit the additional evidence to be led notwithstanding that a witness must be recalled.

(3) The judge may, when granting a motion in terms of this section, adjourn or postpone the trial before permitting the additional evidence to be led.

Evidence in replication.

350A.—(1) The judge may, on a motion of the prosecutor made after the close of the defence evidence and before the prosecutor proceeds to address the judge on the evidence, permit the prosecutor to lead additional evidence, for the purpose of—

(*a*) contradicting evidence, led by the defence, which could not reasonably have been anticipated by the prosecutor; or

(*b*) providing such proof as is mentioned in section 349 of this Act.

(2) The judge may permit the additional evidence to be led notwithstanding that a witness must be recalled.

(3) The judge may, when granting a motion in terms of this section, adjourn or postpone the trial before permitting the additional evidence to be led.".

Offences in connection with lights, reflectors, obstruction, etc., to be provable by one witness.
1967 c. 76.

31. In section 80 of the Road Traffic Regulation Act 1967 (enforcement of certain traffic laws) there shall be inserted after subsection (9) the following subsection—

" (9A) In any proceedings in Scotland for an offence to which this section applies committed in respect of a vehicle to which any of paragraphs (*a*) to (*d*) and (*f*) of subsection (1) above is applicable, it shall be lawful to convict the accused on the evidence of one witness.".

Evidence by letter of request or on commission.

32.—(1) In any criminal proceedings in the High Court or the sheriff court the prosecutor or the defence may, at an appropriate time, apply to a judge of the court in which the trial is to take place (or, if that is not yet known, to a judge of the High Court) for—

(*a*) the issue of a letter of request to a court, or tribunal, exercising jurisdiction in a country or territory outside the United Kingdom, Channel Islands and Isle of Man for the examination of a witness resident in the said country or territory; or

PART II

(*b*) the appointment of a commissioner to examine, at any place in the United Kingdom, Channel Islands, or Isle of Man, a witness who by reason of being ill or infirm is unable to attend the trial diet.

(2) A hearing, as regards any application under subsection (1) above by a party, shall be conducted in chambers but may be dispensed with if the application is not opposed. The application may be granted only if the judge is satisfied that—

(*a*) the evidence which it is averred the witness is able to give is necessary for the proper adjudication of the trial; and

(*b*) there would be no unfairness to the other party were such evidence to be received in the form of the record of an examination conducted by virtue of that subsection.

(3) Any such record as is mentioned in paragraph (*b*) of subsection (2) above shall, without being sworn to by witnesses, be received in evidence in so far as it either accords with the averment mentioned in paragraph (*a*) of that subsection or can be so received without unfairness to either party.

(4) The procedure as regards the foregoing provisions of this section shall be prescribed by Act of Adjournal under the 1975 Act.

(5) In subsection (1) above, " appropriate time " means as regards—

(*a*) solemn proceedings, any time before the oath is administered to the jury;

(*b*) summary proceedings, any time before the first witness is sworn,

or (but only in relation to an application under paragraph (*b*) of that subsection) any time during the course of the trial if the circumstances on which the application is based had not arisen, or would not have merited such application, within the period mentioned in paragraph (*a*), or as the case may be (*b*), of this subsection.

(6) This section is without prejudice to any existing power at common law to adjourn a trial diet to the place where a witness is.

Appeals

Solemn appeals.

33. The provisions of the 1975 Act relating to appeals in solemn proceedings shall have effect as amended by Schedule 2 to this Act.

PART II

Summary appeals.

34. The provisions of the 1975 Act relating to appeals in summary proceedings shall have effect as amended by Schedule 3 to this Act.

Prosecution appeal by bill of advocation.

35. After section 280 of the 1975 Act there shall be inserted the following section—

"Prosecution appeal by bill of advocation.

280A.—(1) Without prejudice to section 76A of this Act, the prosecutor's right to bring a decision under review of the High Court by way of bill of advocation in accordance with existing law and practice shall extend to the review of a decision of any court of solemn jurisdiction.

(2) Where a decision to which a bill of advocation relates is reversed on the review of the decision the prosecutor may, whether or not there has already been a trial diet at which evidence has been led, proceed against the accused by serving him with an indictment containing the charge or charges which were affected by the decision (the wording of which charge or charges shall be as it was immediately before the decision appealed against).".

Appeals from decisions on competency and relevancy in summary proceedings.

36. In section 334 of the 1975 Act (procedure at first diet), after subsection (2) (as substituted by paragraph 54(*b*) of Schedule 7 to this Act) there shall be inserted the following subsections—

"(2A) Without prejudice to any right of appeal under section 442 or 453A of this Act, a party may, with the leave of the court (granted either on the motion of that party or *ex proprio motu*) and in accordance with such procedure as may be prescribed by Act of Adjournal under this Act, appeal to the High Court against a decision of the court of first instance (other than a decision not to grant leave under this subsection) which relates to such objection or denial as is mentioned in subsection (1) above; but such appeal must be taken not later than two days after such decision.

(2B) Where an appeal is taken under subsection (2A) above, the High Court may postpone the trial diet (if one has been fixed) for such period as appears to them to be appropriate and may, if they think fit, direct that such period (or some part of it) shall not count towards any time limit applying in respect of the case.

(2C) If leave to appeal under subsection (2A) above is granted by the court it shall not proceed to trial at once

PART II

under paragraph (*a*) of section 337 of this Act; and paragraph (*b*) of that section shall be construed as requiring sufficient time to be allowed for the appeal to be taken.

(2D) In disposing of an appeal under subsection (2A) above the High Court may affirm the decision of the court of first instance or may remit the case to it with such directions in the matter as they think fit; and where the court of first instance had dismissed the complaint, or any part of it, may reverse that decision and direct that the court of first instance fix a trial diet (if it has not already fixed one as regards so much of the complaint as it has not dismissed.)".

Lord Advocate's reference.

37. After section 263 of the 1975 Act there shall be inserted the following section—

"Lord Advocate's reference.

263A.—(1) Where a person tried on indictment is acquitted of a charge, the Lord Advocate may refer a point of law which has arisen in relation to that charge to the High Court for their opinion; and the Clerk of Justiciary shall send to the person and to any solicitor who acted for the person at the trial, a copy of the reference and intimation of the date fixed by the Court for a hearing.

(2) The person may, not later than seven days before the date so fixed, intimate in writing to the Clerk of Justiciary and to the Lord Advocate either—

(*a*) that he elects to appear personally at the hearing; or

(*b*) that he elects to be represented thereat by counsel;

but, except by leave of the Court on cause shown, (and without prejudice to his right to attend), he shall not appear or be represented at the hearing other than by and in conformity with an election under this subsection.

(3) Where there is no intimation under subsection (2)(*b*) above, the High Court shall appoint counsel to act at the hearing as *amicus curiae*.

(4) The costs of representation elected under subsection (2)(*b*) above or of an appointment under subsection (3) above shall, after being taxed by the Auditor of the Court of Session, be paid by the Lord Advocate.

(5) The opinion on the point referred under subsection (1) above shall not affect the acquittal in the trial.".

Miscellaneous

PART II

Summary trial of wilful fire-raising.

38. In section 291(3) of the 1975 Act (trial of certain offences), after the word " of " there shall be inserted the words " wilful fire-raising,".

Procedure and evidence in trials for treason.

39. The procedure and rules of evidence in proceedings for treason and misprision of treason shall be the same as in proceedings according to the law of Scotland for murder.

PART III

PENALTIES

Previous conviction deemed to be admitted.

40. In section 357(1) of the 1975 Act (laying of previous convictions before court), in paragraph (*c*), for the words from " the judge ", where they occur for the second time, to the end there shall be substituted the words—

" (i) in a case where the plea of guilty is tendered in writing the accused shall be deemed to admit any previous conviction set forth in the notice, unless he expressly denies it in the writing by which that plea is tendered;

(ii) in any other case the judge or the clerk of court shall ask the accused whether he admits the previous conviction,

and if such admission is made or deemed to be made it shall be entered in the record of the proceedings.".

Restriction on passing sentence of imprisonment or detention on person not legally represented.

41.—(1) A court shall not pass a sentence of imprisonment or of detention in respect of any offence, nor impose imprisonment, or detention, under section 396(2) of the 1975 Act in respect of failure to pay a fine, on an accused who is not legally represented in that court and has not been previously sentenced to imprisonment or detention by a court in any part of the United Kingdom, unless the accused either—

(*a*) applied for legal aid and the application was refused on the ground that he was not financially eligible; or

(*b*) having been informed of his right to apply for legal aid, and having had the opportunity, failed to do so.

(2) The court shall, for the purpose of determining whether a person has been previously sentenced to imprisonment or detention by a court in any part of the United Kingdom—

(*a*) disregard a previous sentence of imprisonment which, having been suspended, has not taken effect under section 23 of the Powers of Criminal Courts Act 1973 or under section 19 of the Treatment of Offenders Act (Northern Ireland) 1968;

1973 c. 62.
1968 c. 29 (N.I.).

PART III

(*b*) construe detention as meaning—

(i) in relation to Scotland, detention in a young offenders institution or detention centre;

(ii) in relation to England and Wales, borstal training or detention in a detention centre; and

(iii) in relation to Northern Ireland, detention in a young offenders centre.

(3) Subsection (1) above does not affect the power of a court to pass sentence on any person for an offence the sentence for which is fixed by law.

(4) In this section—

"legal aid" means legal aid for the purposes of any part of the proceedings before the court;

"legally represented" means represented by counsel or a solicitor at some stage after the accused is found guilty and before he is dealt with as referred to in subsection (1) above.

Restriction on passing sentence of imprisonment on person not previously so dealt with.

42.—(1) A court shall not pass a sentence of imprisonment on a person of or over twenty-one years of age who has not been previously sentenced to imprisonment or detention by a court in any part of the United Kingdom unless the court considers that no other method of dealing with him is appropriate; and for the purpose of determining whether any other method of dealing with such a person is appropriate the court shall obtain (from an officer of a local authority or otherwise) such information as it can about the offender's circumstances; and it shall also take into account any information before it concerning the offender's character and physical and mental condition.

(2) Where a court of summary jurisdiction passes a sentence of imprisonment on any such person as is mentioned in subsection (1) above, the court shall state the reason for its opinion that no other method of dealing with him is appropriate, and shall have that reason entered in the record of the proceedings.

(3) Subsections (2) and (3) of section 41 of this Act shall apply for the purposes of this section as they apply for the purposes of that section.

Punishment for murder.

43. For section 205 of the 1975 Act there shall be substituted the following sections—

"Punishment for murder.

205.—(1) Subject to subsections (2) and (3) below, a person convicted of murder shall be sentenced to imprisonment for life.

(2) Where a person convicted of murder is under the age of 18 years he shall not be sentenced to

imprisonment for life but to be detained without limit of time and shall be liable to be detained in such place, and under such conditions, as the Secretary of State may direct. PART III

(3) Where a person convicted of murder has attained the age of 18 years but is under the age of 21 years he shall not be sentenced to imprisonment for life but to be detained in a young offenders institution and shall be liable to be detained for life.

Recommendation as to minimum period of detention for person convicted of murder.

205A.—(1) On sentencing any person convicted of murder a judge may make a recommendation as to the minimum period which should elapse before, under section 61 of the Criminal Justice Act 1967, the Secretary of State releases that person on licence.

(2) When making a recommendation under subsection (1) above, the judge shall state his reasons for so recommending.

(3) Notwithstanding the proviso to subsection (1) of section 228 of this Act it shall be competent to appeal under paragraph (*b*) or (*c*) of that subsection against a recommendation made under subsection (1) above; and for the purposes of such appeal (including the High Court's power of disposal under section 254(3)(*b*) of this Act) the recommendation shall be deemed part of the sentence passed on conviction.".

Detention and release on licence of children convicted on indictment.

44. For section 206 of the 1975 Act there shall be substituted the following section—

"Detention and release on licence of children convicted on indictment.

206.—(1) Subject to section 205 of this Act, where a child is convicted and the court is of the opinion that no other method of dealing with him is appropriate, it may sentence him to be detained for a period which it shall specify in the sentence; and the child shall during that period be liable to be detained in such place and on such conditions as the Secretary of State may direct.

(2) Subject to subsection (3) below, the Secretary of State may release on licence, on such conditions as may for the time being be specified in the licence, a person detained under subsection (1) above.

(3) Where a person has been sentenced under subsection (1) above to be detained for a period exceeding 18 months, the Secretary of State—

(*a*) shall not release him on licence under subsection (2) above except on the recommendation of the Parole Board for Scotland (in

PART III

this section referred to as " the Board "); and

(*b*) shall consult the Board with regard to the inclusion or subsequent insertion of any condition in the licence or the variation or cancellation of any such condition ; but for the purposes of this paragraph the Secretary of State shall be treated as having consulted the Board about a proposal to include, insert, vary or cancel a condition in any case if he has consulted the Board about the implementation of proposals of that description generally or in that class of case.

(4) A licence granted under subsection (2) above shall, unless previously revoked under subsection (5) below, remain in force until the expiry of the period of—

(*a*) detention specified by the court under subsection (1) above ; or

(*b*) 12 months from the date of release under the licence,

whichever is the later.

(5) The Secretary of State may—

(*a*) on the recommendation of the Board ; or

(*b*) at his own instance, where it appears to him to be in the public interest to do so before consultation with the Board is practicable,

revoke a licence granted under subsection (2) above and recall the person released under the licence to a place in which the Secretary of State directs that he should be detained ; and on such revocation, the person shall be liable to be detained in pursuance of his sentence, and, if at large, shall be deemed to be unlawfully at large.

(6) The Secretary of State shall inform a person recalled under subsection (5) above of the reasons for his recall, so that the person may make representations in writing with respect to his recall to the Board ; and the Board may, on receipt of such representations, require the Secretary of State to release him on licence forthwith.

(7) Subject to subsection (6) above, a person detained in pursuance of subsection (5) above shall

PART III

remain in detention until the expiry of the period of—

(a) detention specified by the court under subsection (1) above; or

(b) 3 months from the date of the commencement of his detention in pursuance of the said subsection (5), whichever is the later:

Provided that the Secretary of State may, at any time before the expiry of the period referred to in paragraph (a) above, again release him on licence.".

Detention of young offenders.

45.—(1) For section 207 of the 1975 Act there shall be substituted the following provision—

"Detention of young offenders.

207.—(1) It shall not be competent to impose imprisonment on a person under 21 years of age.

(2) Subject to section 205(2) and (3) of this Act and to subsections (3) and (4) below a court may impose detention (whether by way of sentence or otherwise) on a person, who is not less than 16 but under 21 years of age, where but for subsection (1) above the court would have power to impose a period of imprisonment; and the period of detention imposed under this section on any person shall not exceed the maximum period of imprisonment which might otherwise have been imposed.

(3) The court shall not under subsection (2) above impose detention on a person unless it is of the opinion that no other method of dealing with him is appropriate; and the court shall state its reasons for that opinion, and, except in the case of the High Court, those reasons shall be entered in the record of proceedings.

(4) To enable the court to form an opinion under subsection (3) above, it shall obtain (from an officer of a local authority or otherwise) such information as it can about the offender's circumstances; and it shall also take into account any information before it concerning the offender's character and physical and mental condition.

(5) Subject to subsections (6) and (8) below—

(a) in a case where a court by way of sentence imposes detention, under subsection (2) above, on a male person for a period of at

PART III

least 28 days but not exceeding 4 months the court shall order that the detention be in a detention centre ; and

(*b*) in any other case it shall order that the detention be in a young offenders institution.

(6) Where detention in a detention centre would be required by subsection (5) above but the court is of the opinion that—

(*a*) the convicted person is physically or mentally unfit to be detained in a detention centre ; or

(*b*) for any special reason, which the court shall state and which shall, except in the case of the High Court, be entered in the record of the proceedings, a young offenders institution is a more appropriate place of detention,

it may under this subsection order that the detention be in a young offenders institution.

(7) Where detention imposed under subsection (5) above is (either or both)—

(*a*) for a period of less than 28 days ;

(*b*) imposed other than by way of sentence,

but the convicted person is already detained in a detention centre, the detention under the said subsection (5) shall, notwithstanding the terms of the order made under that subsection by the court, be in a detention centre.

(8) Periods of detention imposed at the same time and ordered to be consecutive shall, for the purposes of this section, be treated as a single period of detention.

(9) Where a person is serving a period of detention in a detention centre when a period of detention is ordered which is—

(*a*) consecutive to the period being served and the periods together total more than 5 months ; or

(*b*) concurrent with the period being served and is for more than 5 months,

the convicted person shall, notwithstanding the terms of any order made under subsection (5) above, be transferred to a young offenders institution to serve the remainder of that total period or as the case may be of those concurrent periods.

(10) Where the Secretary of State is satisfied that a person is physically or mentally unfit to be detained in a detention centre, he may transfer such person to a young offenders institution.

(11) Section 20 of the Prisons (Scotland) Act 1952 (remission for good conduct) and sections 59 to 62 and 64 of the Criminal Justice Act 1967 (release on licence) shall apply to a person sentenced under this section as those enactments apply to a person sentenced to a period of imprisonment." ;

and the same provision shall (with the appropriate section number) be substituted for section 415 of the 1975 Act, except that in subsection (2) of the provision the words " section 205(2) and (3) of this Act and to " shall be omitted.

(2) Sections 10 (transfer to prison of persons over 21), 12 (supervision of persons released from young offenders institutions) and 51 (interpretation) of the Criminal Justice (Scotland) Act 1963 shall have effect subject to the amendments set out in Schedule 5 to this Act. 1963 c. 39.

(3) In the 1975 Act, sections 204 and 414 (Borstal training) and sections 209 and 418 (detention in detention centre) shall cease to have effect.

(4) Without prejudice to any specific amendment made by this Act, in Scotland a reference in any enactment to which this subsection applies—

(*a*) to a Borstal institution, shall be construed as a reference to a young offenders institution ; and

(*b*) to a period of training in a Borstal institution, shall be construed as a reference to a period of detention in a young offenders institution.

(5) The enactments to which subsection (4) above applies are—

(*a*) any Act passed before, or during the same session as, this Act ; and

(*b*) any subordinate legislation made before the commencement of this Act ;

and in this subsection " Act " and " subordinate legislation " have the same meanings as in the Interpretation Act 1978. 1978 c. 13.

Increase of certain penalties and other sums.

46.—(1) In the 1975 Act—

(*a*) in section 186(2)(*a*) (breach of probation order), for the words " £20 " there shall be substituted the words " £50 " ;

PART III

(*b*) in section 312(*z*) (form of charge in complaint) for the words " £25 " there shall be substituted the words " £200 ";

(*c*) in section 344 (1) (penalty for contempt), for the words " £25 " and "20 days " there shall be substituted respectively the words " £50 " and " 21 days ";

(*d*) in section 387(2)(*a*) (breach of probation order), for the words " £20 " there shall be substituted the words " £50 ";

(*e*) in section 435(*e*) (expenses), for the words " £12 " there shall be substituted the words " £200 " and for the words " £3 ", in both places where they occur, there shall be substituted the words " £50 "; and

(*f*) in section 453(3) (expenses to appellant on conviction being set aside), for the words " £5.25 " there shall be substituted the words " £20 ".

(2) In section 193 of the 1975 Act (power to mitigate penalties), in subsection (2) for the words " an amount of £150 ", and in subsection (3) for the words "the amount of £150 ", there shall be substituted in each case the words " the prescribed sum within the meaning of section 289B of this Act ".

Application to solemn procedure of summary procedure provisions relating to fines.

47. For section 194 of the 1975 Act there shall be substituted the following section—

"Application of summary procedure provisions relating to fines.

194.—(1) The provisions of Part II of this Act specified in subsection (2) below shall, subject to any necessary modifications, apply in relation to solemn proceedings as they apply in relation to summary proceedings.

(2) The provisions mentioned in subsection (1) above are—

section 395(1) (means of offender to be taken into account);

section 395A (power to remit fines);

section 396 (time for payment);

section 397 (further time for payment);

section 398 (reasons for default);

section 399 (payment by instalments);

section 400 (supervision pending payment of fine);

section 401(2) and (3) (supplementary provisions);

section 403 (transfer of fine orders);

PART III

section 404 (action of clerk of court on transfer of fine order);

section 406 (substitution of custody for imprisonment where child defaults on fine);

section 407 (maximum period of imprisonment for non-payment of fine);

section 408 (discharge from imprisonment to be specified);

section 409 (payment of fine in part by prisoner);

section 411 (recovery by civil diligence);

Schedule 7 (application of sums paid as part of fine under section 409).".

Enforcement of High Court fine by sheriff.

48. In section 196 of the 1975 Act (fines may be enforced in other district), the existing words shall be subsection (1) of that section and after that subsection there shall be inserted the following subsection—

"(2) A fine imposed by the High Court shall be remitted for enforcement to, and shall be enforceable as if it had been imposed by—

(*a*) where the person upon whom the fine was imposed resides in Scotland, the sheriff for the district where that person resides;

(*b*) where that person resides outwith Scotland, the sheriff before whom he was brought for examination in relation to the offence for which the fine was imposed.".

Power to remit fines.

49. After section 395 of the 1975 Act there shall be inserted the following section—

"Power to remit fines.

395A.—(1) A fine may at any time be remitted in whole or in part by—

(*a*) in a case where a transfer of fine order under section 403 of this Act is effective and the court by which payment is enforceable is, in terms of the order, a court of summary jurisdiction in Scotland, that court; or

(*b*) in any other case, the court which imposed the fine or (where that court was the High Court) by which payment was first enforceable.

(2) Where the court remits the whole or part of a fine after imprisonment has been imposed under section 396(2) or (4) of this Act, it shall also remit

PART III

the whole period of imprisonment or, as the case may be, reduce the period by an amount which bears the same proportion to the whole period as the amount remitted bears to the whole fine.

(3) The power conferred by subsection (1) above shall be exerciseable without requiring the attendance of the accused.".

Maximum period of imprisonment for non-payment of fine in summary proceedings.

50. In section 407 of the 1975 Act (imprisonment for non-payment of fine), for subsection (1) there shall be substituted the following subsections—

" (1) Subject to sections 396 to 401 of this Act—

(*a*) a court of summary jurisdiction may, when imposing a fine, impose a period of imprisonment in default of payment; or

(*b*) where no order has been made under paragraph (*a*) above and a person fails to pay a fine, or any part or instalment of a fine, by the time ordered by the court (or, where section 396(2) of this Act applies, immediately) the court may impose a period of imprisonment for such failure,

whether or not the fine is imposed under an enactment which makes provision for its enforcement or recovery.

(1A) Subject to the following subsections of this section, the maximum period of imprisonment which may be imposed under subsection (1) above or for failure to find caution, shall be as follows—

Amount of Fine or of Caution	*Maximum Period of Imprisonment*
Not exceeding £25	7 days
Exceeding £25 but not exceeding £50 ...	14 days
Exceeding £50 but not exceeding £200 ...	30 days
Exceeding £200 but not exceeding £500 ...	60 days
Exceeding £500 but not exceeding £1,000	90 days
Exceeding £1,000 but not exceeding £2,500	6 months
Exceeding £2,500 but not exceeding £5,000	9 months
Exceeding £5,000	12 months.

(1B) Where an offender is fined on the same day before the same court for offences charged in the same complaint or in separate complaints, the amount of the fine shall, for the purposes of this section, be taken to be the total of the fines imposed.

PART III

(1C) Where a court has imposed a period of imprisonment in default of payment of a fine, and—

(*a*) an instalment of the fine is not paid at the time ordered ; or

(*b*) part only of the fine has been paid within the time allowed for payment,

the offender shall be liable to imprisonment for a period which bears to the period so imposed the same proportion, as nearly as may be, as the amount outstanding at the time when warrant is issued for imprisonment of the offender in default bears to the original fine.

(1D) Where no period of imprisonment in default of payment of a fine has been imposed and—

(*a*) an instalment of the fine is not paid at the time ordered ; or

(*b*) part only of the fine has been paid within the time allowed for payment,

the offender shall be liable to imprisonment for a maximum period which bears, as nearly as may be, the same proportion to the maximum period of imprisonment which could have been imposed by virtue of the Table in subsection (1A) above in default of payment of the original fine as the amount outstanding at the time when he appears before the court bears to the original fine.".

Execution in different parts of United Kingdom of warrants for imprisonment for non-payment of fine.

51. After section 38 of the Criminal Law Act 1977 there shall be inserted the following section—

"Execution in different parts of United Kingdom of warrants for imprisonment for non-payment of fine.

38A.—(1) Subject to subsection (6) below, a person against whom an extract conviction is issued in Scotland for imprisonment in default of payment of a fine may be arrested—

(*a*) in England and Wales, by any constable acting within his police area ;

(*b*) in Northern Ireland, by any member of the Royal Ulster Constabulary or the Royal Ulster Constabulary Reserve ;

and subsections (4) and (5) of section 159 of the Magistrates' Courts Act (Northern Ireland) 1964 (execution without possession of the warrant and execution on Sunday) shall apply to the execution in Northern Ireland of any such extract conviction as those subsections apply in relation to the execution of a warrant for arrest.

PART III

(2) Subject to subsection (6) below, a person against whom there has been issued in England, Wales or Northern Ireland a warrant committing him to prison in default of payment of a sum adjudged to be paid by a conviction may be arrested in Scotland, by any constable appointed for a police area, in like manner as if the warrant were an extract conviction for imprisonment issued in Scotland in default of payment of a fine.

(3) A person arrested by virtue of subsection (1) above under an extract conviction or by virtue of subsection (2) above under a warrant of commitment may be detained under it in any prison in the part of the United Kingdom in which he was arrested; and while so detained he shall be treated for all purposes as if he were detained under a warrant of commitment or extract conviction issued in that part of the United Kingdom.

(4) An extract conviction or a warrant of commitment may be executed by virtue of this section whether or not it has been endorsed under section 4 of the Summary Jurisdiction (Process) Act 1881 or under section 27 of the Petty Sessions (Ireland) Act 1851.

(5) In this section—

'fine' includes any sum treated by any enactment as a fine for the purposes of its enforcement and any sum to be found as caution;

'imprisonment' includes, in the case of a person who is under the age of 21 years, detention;

'part of the United Kingdom' means England and Wales, Scotland or Northern Ireland;

'prison' means—

(i) in the case of a person who is under the age of 21 years arrested in Scotland, a young offenders institution; and

(ii) in the case of a person under that age arrested in Northern Ireland, a young offenders centre; and

'sum adjudged to be paid by a conviction' has the meaning given by section 150(3) of the Magistrates' Courts Act 1980 or, in Northern Ireland, section 169(2) of the Magistrates' Courts (Northern Ireland) Act 1964.

(6) This section shall not apply to the arrest of persons under the age of 17 years.".

PART III

Recovery of fine or caution by civil diligence.

52. Where proceedings by civil diligence for recovery of a fine or caution are adopted, imprisonment for non-payment of the fine or for failure to find such caution shall remain competent, and such proceedings by civil diligence may be authorised after the court has imposed imprisonment for (or in the event of) the non-payment or the failure but before imprisonment has followed such imposition; and accordingly in section 411 of the 1975 Act—

(*a*) subsection (2) shall cease to have effect; and

(*b*) in the proviso to subsection (3), for the words " court has imposed imprisonment in default of " there shall be substituted the words " offender has been imprisoned in consequence of his having defaulted in ".

Availability of probation after deferred sentence.

53.—(1) In section 384(1) of the 1975 Act (probation), after the word " conviction " there shall be inserted the words—

" (except in a case to which section 432 of this Act applies) ".

(2) In section 432 of the said Act (deferred sentence), at the end there shall be added the words—

" ; and the fact that the accused has been convicted shall not prevent the court from making, in due course, a probation order under section 384 of this Act.".

Dealing with person who commits further offence while sentence is deferred.

54. In each of sections 219 and 432 of the 1975 Act (deferred sentence), the existing words shall be subsection (1) of the section and after that subsection there shall be inserted the following subsections—

" (2) If it appears to the court by which sentence on a person has been deferred under subsection (1) above that that person has been convicted, during the period of deferment, by a court in any part of Great Britain of an offence committed during that period and has been dealt with for that offence, the first mentioned court may issue a warrant for the arrest of that person, or may, instead of issuing such a warrant in the first instance, issue a citation requiring him to appear before it at such time as may be specified in the citation; and on his appearance or on his being brought before the court it may deal with him in any manner in which it would be competent for it to deal with him on the expiry of the period of deferment.

(3) Where a court which has deferred sentence under subsection (1) above on a person convicts that person of another offence during the period of deferment, it may deal with him for the original offence in any manner in which it would be

PART III

competent for it to deal with him on the expiry of the period of deferment, as well as for the offence committed during the said period.".

Disqualification and endorsement where orders for probation or for absolute discharge are made. 1972 c. 20.

55. In the Road Traffic Act 1972, in each of sections 93 (disqualification on conviction of certain offences) and 101 (endorsement of licences), there shall be added at the end the following subsection—

"(8) Where a person is charged with any offence in Scotland mentioned in this section, and the court makes an order in respect of that offence under section 182 or 383 (absolute discharge) or 183 or 384 (probation) of the Criminal Procedure (Scotland) Act 1975, then, for the purposes of this section, he shall be treated as if he had been convicted of such an offence and section 191 or, as the case may be, section 392 of that Act shall not apply.".

Penalties for drunkenness. 1903 c. 25.

56.—(1) In section 70 of the Licensing (Scotland) Act 1903 (penalties for drunkenness, etc.)—

(*a*) in the first paragraph of subsection (1) for the words from " and may be taken " to the end of that paragraph there shall be substituted the words " and shall be liable on summary conviction to a fine not exceeding £50 " ;

(*b*) in the second paragraph of that subsection for the words from " forty " to the end of that paragraph there shall be substituted the words " £50 " ;

(*c*) after that subsection there shall be inserted the following subsection—

" (1A) A constable may arrest without warrant any person who he has reasonable grounds for suspecting is committing an offence under subsection (1) above." ; and

(*d*) in subsection (2) for the words from " forty " to the end of the first sentence there shall be substituted the words " £50 ".

1892 c. 25.

(2) Section 382 of the Burgh Police (Scotland) Act 1892 shall cease to have effect.

Penalty for second conviction of assault on constable. 1967 c. 77.

57. In section 41(1)(ii) of the Police (Scotland) Act 1967 (assaults on constables, etc.), at the end there shall be added the words " or to a fine not exceeding the prescribed sum within the meaning of section 289B of the Criminal Procedure (Scotland) Act 1975, or to both.".

Part IV

Compensation by Offenders

Compensation order against convicted person.

58.—(1) Subject to subsection (3) below, where a person is convicted of an offence the court, instead of or in addition to dealing with him in any other way, may make an order (in this Act referred to as " a compensation order ") requiring him to pay compensation for any personal injury, loss or damage caused (whether directly or indirectly) by the acts which constituted the offence:

Provided that it shall not be competent for a court to make a compensation order—

(*a*) where, under section 182 of the 1975 Act, it makes an order discharging him absolutely;

(*b*) where, under section 183 of that Act, it makes a probation order; or

(*c*) at the same time as, under section 219 or 432 of that Act, it defers sentence.

(2) Where, in the case of an offence involving the dishonest appropriation, or the unlawful taking and using, of property or a contravention of section 175(1) of the Road Traffic Act 1972 (taking motor vehicle without authority etc.) the property is recovered, but has been damaged while out of the owner's possession, that damage (however and by whomsoever it was in fact caused) shall be treated for the purposes of subsection (1) above as having been caused by the acts which constituted the offence.

1972 c. 20.

(3) No compensation order shall be made in respect of—

(*a*) loss suffered in consequence of the death of any person; or

(*b*) injury, loss or damage due to an accident arising out of the presence of a motor vehicle on a road, except such damage as is treated, by virtue of subsection (2) above, as having been caused by the convicted person's acts.

Amount of compensation order.

59.—(1) In determining whether to make a compensation order against any person, and in determining the amount to be paid by any person under such order, the court shall take into consideration his means so far as known to the court:

Provided that where the person is serving, or is to serve, a period of imprisonment or detention no account shall be taken, in assessing such means, of earnings contingent upon his obtaining employment after release.

PART IV

(2) In solemn proceedings there shall be no limit on the amount which may be awarded under a compensation order.

(3) In summary proceedings—

(a) a sheriff, or a stipendiary magistrate appointed under section 5 of the District Courts (Scotland) Act 1975, shall have power to make a compensation order awarding in respect of each offence an amount not exceeding the prescribed sum (within the meaning of section 289B of the Criminal Procedure (Scotland) Act 1975);

1975 c. 20.

1975 c. 21.

(b) a judge of a district court (other than such stipendiary magistrate) shall have power to make a compensation order awarding in respect of each offence an amount not exceeding £200.

Payment under compensation order.

60.—(1) Payment of any amount under a compensation order shall be made to the clerk of the court who shall account for the amount to the person entitled thereto.

(2) Only the court shall have power to enforce a compensation order.

Guidance as to whether compensation order or fine should be preferred.

61. Where a court considers that in respect of an offence it would be appropriate to impose a fine and to make a compensation order but the convicted person has insufficient means to pay both an appropriate fine and an appropriate amount in compensation the court should prefer a compensation order.

Precedence of compensation order over fine.

62. Where a convicted person has both been fined and had a compensation order made against him in respect of the same offence or different offences in the same proceedings, a payment by the convicted person shall first be applied in satisfaction of the compensation order.

Appeal as regards compensation order.

63.—(1) For the purposes of any appeal or review, a compensation order is a sentence.

(2) Where a compensation order has been made against a person, a payment made to the court in respect of the order shall be retained until the determination of any appeal in relation to the order.

Review of compensation order.

64. Without prejudice to the power contained in section 395A of the 1975 Act, (as applied by section 66 of this Act), at any time before a compensation order has been complied with or fully complied with—

(a) in a case where, as respects the compensation order, a transfer of fine order under section 403 of the 1975

Act (as applied by the said section 66) is effective and the court by which the compensation order is enforceable is in terms of the transfer of fine order a court of summary jurisdiction in Scotland, that court; or

(*b*) in any other case, the court which made the compensation order or (where that court was the High Court) by which the order was first enforceable,

may, on the application of the person against whom the compensation order was made, discharge the compensation order, or reduce the amount that remains to be paid, if it appears to the court either that the injury, loss or damage in respect of which the compensation order was made has been held in civil proceedings to be less than it was taken to be for the purposes of the compensation order or that property the loss of which is reflected in the compensation order has been recovered.

Acts of Adjournal.

65. The High Court's power to make Acts of Adjournal under sections 282 and 457 of the 1975 Act shall include power to make rules with regard to any of the provisions of this Part of this Act, including rules relating to the award and payment, by compensation orders, of sums to persons under any legal disability.

Application of provisions relating to fines to enforcement of compensation orders.

66.—(1) The provisions of the 1975 Act specified in subsection (2) below shall, subject to any necessary modifications and to the qualifications mentioned in that subsection, apply in relation to compensation orders as they apply in relation to fines; and sections 91 of the Magistrates' Courts Act 1980 and 104B of the Magistrates' Courts Act (Northern Ireland) 1964 shall be construed accordingly.

1980 c. 43.

1964 c. 21. (N.I.).

(2) The provisions mentioned in subsection (1) above are—

section 194 (application to solemn procedure of summary procedure provisions relating to fines);

section 196 (fines etc., may be enforced in other district);

section 395(2) to (7) (application of money found on offender);

section 395A (power to remit fines), with the omission of the words " or (4) " in subsection (2) of that section;

section 396 (time for payment) with the omission of the words from " unless " to " its decision " in subsection (4) and of subsection (5) of that section;

section 397 (further time for payment);

PART IV

section 398 (reasons for default);

section 399 (payment by instalments);

section 400 (supervision pending payment of fine);

section 401 (supplementary provisions), except that subsection (1) of that section shall not apply in relation to compensation orders made in solemn proceedings;

section 402 (fines etc., may be enforced in another district);

section 403 (transfer of fine orders);

section 404 (action of clerk of court on transfer of fine order);

section 406 (substitution of custody for imprisonment where child defaults on fine);

section 407(1)(*b*), (1A), (1B), (1D), (2) and (4) (maximum period of imprisonment for non-payment of fine):

Provided that—

(*a*) a court may impose imprisonment in respect of a fine and decline to impose imprisonment in respect of a compensation order but not *vice versa*; and

(*b*) where a court imposes imprisonment both in respect of a fine and of a compensation order the amounts in respect of which imprisonment is imposed shall, for the purposes of the said subsection (1A), be aggregated;

section 408 (discharge from imprisonment to be specified);

section 409 (payment of fine in part by prisoner);

section 411 (recovery by civil diligence); and

Schedule 7 (application of sums paid as part of fine under section 409).

Effect of compensation order on subsequent award of damages in civil proceedings.

67.—(1) This section shall have effect where a compensation order has been made in favour of any person in respect of any injury, loss or damage and a claim by him in civil proceedings for damages in respect thereof subsequently falls to be determined.

(2) The damages in the civil proceedings shall be assessed without regard to the order; but where the whole or part of the amount awarded by the order has been paid, the damages awarded in the civil proceedings shall be restricted to the amount (if any) by which, as so assessed, they exceed the amount paid under the order.

(3) Where the whole or part of the amount awarded by the order remains unpaid and damages are awarded in a judgment in the civil proceedings, then, unless the person against whom the order was made has ceased to be liable to pay the amount unpaid (whether in consequence of an appeal, or of his imprisonment for default or otherwise), the court shall direct that the judgment—

(a) if it is for an amount not exceeding the amount unpaid under the order, shall not be enforced; or

(b) if it is for an amount exceeding the amount unpaid under the order, shall not be enforced except to the extent that it exceeds the amount unpaid,

without the leave of the court.

PART V

SPORTING EVENTS: CONTROL OF ALCOHOL ETC.

Designation of sports grounds and sporting events.

68.—(1) The Secretary of State may for the purposes of this Part of this Act by order designate—

(a) a sports ground or a class of sports ground;

(b) a sporting event, or a class of sporting event, at that ground or at any of that class of ground:

Provided that a sporting event at which all the participants take part without financial or material reward and to which all spectators are admitted free of charge shall not be subject to an order under this section; but this proviso is without prejudice to the order's validity as respects any other sporting event.

(2) The power to make an order under subsection (1) above shall be exercisable by statutory instrument which shall be subject to annulment in pursuance of a resolution of either House of Parliament.

Alcohol on vehicle travelling to or from sporting event.

69. Where a public service vehicle is being operated for the principal purpose of conveying passengers to or from a designated sporting event, then—

(a) any person in possession of alcohol on the vehicle shall be guilty of an offence and liable on summary conviction to imprisonment for a period not exceeding 60 days or a fine not exceeding £200 or both;

(b) if alcohol is being carried on the vehicle and the vehicle is on hire to a person, he shall, subject to section 71

PART V

of this Act, be guilty of an offence and liable on summary conviction to a fine not exceeding £200 ; and

(*c*) any person who is drunk on the vehicle shall be guilty of an offence and liable on summary conviction to a fine not exceeding £50.

Liability of vehicle operator and his employees and agents.
1976 c. 66.

70. Notwithstanding section 92 of the Licensing (Scotland) Act 1976 (restriction on carriage of alcoholic liquor in crates on contract carriages), but subject to section 71 of this Act, if the operator of a public service vehicle which is being operated as mentioned in section 69 of this Act, either by himself or by his employee or agent permits alcohol to be carried on the vehicle, the operator and, as the case may be, the employee or agent shall be guilty of an offence and liable on summary conviction to a fine not exceding £200.

Defences in connection with carriage of alcohol.

71. Where a person is charged with an offence under section 69(*b*) or 70 of this Act, it shall be a defence for him to prove that the alcohol was carried on the vehicle without his consent or connivance and that he did all he reasonably could to prevent such carriage.

Possession of container at sporting event.

72.—(1) Any person who—

(*a*) is in possession of a controlled container in ; or

(*b*) while in possession of a controlled container, attempts to enter,

the relevant area of a designated sports ground at any time during the period of a designated sporting event, shall be guilty of an offence and liable on summary conviction to imprisonment for a period not exceeding 60 days or to a fine not exceeding £200 or both.

(2) In subsection (1) above, the term " controlled container " means any bottle, can or other portable container, whether open or sealed, which is, or was in its original manufactured state, capable of containing liquid and is made from such material or is of such construction, or is so adapted, that if it were thrown at or propelled against a person it would be capable of causing some injury to that person ; but the term does not include a container holding a medicinal product for a medicinal purpose.

(3) In subsection (2) above, " medicinal product " and " medicinal purpose " have the meanings assigned to those terms by section 130 of the Medicines Act 1968.

1968 c. 67.

PART V

Possession of alcohol at sporting event.

73. Any person who—

(*a*) is in possession of alcohol in; or

(*b*) while in possession of alcohol, attempts to enter,

the relevant area of a designated sports ground at any time during the period of a designated sporting event, shall be guilty of an offence and liable on summary conviction to imprisonment for a period not exceeding 60 days or to a fine not exceeding £200 or both.

Drunkenness at sporting event.

74. Any person who—

(*a*) is drunk in; or

(*b*) while drunk, attempts to enter,

the relevant area of a designated sports ground at any time during the period of a designated sporting event shall be guilty of an offence and liable on summary conviction to a fine not exceeding £50.

Police powers of enforcement.

75. For the purpose of enforcing the provisions of this Part of this Act, a constable shall have the power without warrant—

(*a*) to enter a designated sports ground at any time during the period of a designated sporting event;

(*b*) to search a person who he has reasonable grounds to suspect is committing or has committed an offence under this Part of this Act;

(*c*) to stop and search a vehicle where he has reasonable grounds to suspect that an offence under section 69 or 70 of this Act is being or has been committed;

(*d*) to arrest a person who he has reasonable grounds to suspect is committing or has committed an offence under this Part of this Act;

(*e*) to seize and detain—

(i) with its contents (if any), a controlled container as defined in section 72(2) of this Act; or

(ii) with its contents, any other container if he has reasonable grounds to suspect that those contents are or include alcohol.

Presumption as to contents of container.

76.—(1) For the purposes of any trial in connection with an alleged contravention of any provision of this Part of this Act, any liquid contained in a container (sealed or open) shall, subject to subsection (2) below, be presumed to conform to the description of the liquid on the container.

PART V

1976 c. 66.

(2) Subsections (3) to (6) of section 127 of the Licensing (Scotland) Act 1976 (right of accused to challenge presumption as to contents) shall apply in relation to subsection (1) above as they apply in relation to subsection (2) of that section.

Interpretation of Part V.

77. In this Part of this Act, unless the context otherwise requires—

" advertised " means announced in any written or printed document or in any broadcast announcement;

1976 c. 66.

" alcohol " means alcoholic liquor as defined in section 139 of the Licensing (Scotland) Act 1976;

" designated " means designated by the Secretary of State by order under section 68 of this Act;

" period of a designated sporting event " means the period commencing two hours before the start and ending one hour after the end of a designated sporting event, except that where the event is advertised as to start at a particular time but is delayed or postponed it includes, and where for any reason an event does not take place it means, the period commencing two hours before and ending one hour after, that particular time;

1980 c. 34.

" public service vehicle " has the like meaning as in Part I of the Transport Act 1980 and " operator " in relation to such a vehicle means—

(*a*) the driver if he owns the vehicle; and

(*b*) in any other case the person for whom the driver works (whether under a contract of employment or any other description of contract personally to do work);

" relevant area " means any part of a sports ground—

(*a*) to which spectators attending a designated sporting event are granted access on payment; or

(*b*) from which a designated sporting event may be viewed directly;

" sporting event " means any physical competitive activity at a sports ground, and includes any such activity which has been advertised as to, but does not, take place; and

" sports ground " means any place whatsoever which is designed, or is capable of being adapted, for the holding of sporting events in respect of which spectators are accommodated.

PART VI

MISCELLANEOUS AND GENERAL

78.—(1) Subject to subsection (2) below, any person who, without reasonable excuse, wilfully or recklessly destroys or damages any property belonging to another shall be guilty of the offence of vandalism. Vandalism.

(2) It shall not be competent to charge acts which constitute the offence of wilful fire-raising as vandalism under this section.

(3) Any person convicted of the offence of vandalism shall be liable on summary conviction—

(*a*) in the district court, to imprisonment for a term not exceeding 60 days, or to a fine not exceeding £200, or to both;

(*b*) in the sheriff court—

(i) for a first such offence, to imprisonment for a term not exceeding 3 months, or to a fine not exceeding the prescribed sum (within the meaning of section 289B of the 1975 Act), or to both; and

(ii) for any subsequent such offence, to imprisonment for a term not exceeding 6 months, or to the fine mentioned in sub-paragraph (i) above, or to both.

79. After section 27A of the Social Work (Scotland) Act 1968 there shall be inserted the following section— Grants in respect of hostel accommodation for persons under supervision. 1968 c. 49.

"Grants in respect of hostel accommodation for persons under supervision.

27B. The Secretary of State may make to a local authority grants of such amount and subject to such conditions as he may with the consent of the Treasury determine in respect of expenditure incurred by the authority under this Act in—

(*a*) providing; or

(*b*) contributing by way of grant under section 10(3) of this Act to the provision by a voluntary organisation of,

residential accommodation wholly or mainly for the persons mentioned in sub-paragraphs (i) and (ii) of section 27(1)(*b*) of this Act.".

80.—(1) Subject to the provisions of this section, a homosexual act in private shall not be an offence provided that the parties consent thereto and have attained the age of twenty-one years. Homosexual offences.

(2) An act which would otherwise be treated for the purposes of this Act as being done in private shall not be so treated if done—

(*a*) when more than two persons take part or are present or

PART VI

(*b*) in a lavatory to which the public have, or are permitted to have, access whether on payment or otherwise.

(3) A male person who is suffering from mental deficiency which is of such a nature or degree that he is incapable of living an independent life or of guarding himself against serious exploitation cannot in law give any consent which, by virtue of subsection (1) above, would prevent a homosexual act from being an offence ; but a person shall not be convicted on account of the incapacity of such a male person to consent, of an offence consisting of such an act if he proves that he did not know and had no reason to suspect that male person to be suffering from such mental deficiency.

1960 c. 61. (4) Section 97 of the Mental Health (Scotland) Act 1960 (prohibition on men on the staff of a hospital, or otherwise having responsibility for mental patients, having sexual intercourse with women patients) shall have effect as if any reference therein to having unlawful sexual intercourse with a woman included a reference to committing a homosexual act.

1955 c. 18. 1955 c. 19. 1957 c. 53. (5) Subsection (1) above shall not prevent a homosexual act from being an offence under any provision of the Army Act 1955, the Air Force Act 1955 or the Naval Discipline Act 1957.

(6) In this section, " a homosexual act " means sodomy or an act of gross indecency by one male person with another male person.

(7) Subject to the provisions of subsection (3) above, it shall be an offence to commit or to be party to the commission of, or to procure or attempt to procure the commission of a homosexual act—

(*a*) otherwise than in private ;

(*b*) without the consent of both parties to the act ;

(*c*) with a person under the age of twenty-one years ; or

(*d*) where the act is committed on board a United Kingdom merchant ship, wherever it may be, by a male person who is a member of the crew of that ship with another male person who is a member of the crew of that ship or any other United Kingdom merchant ship.

(8) In this section—

" member of the crew " in relation to a ship, includes the master of the ship ;

" United Kingdom merchant ship " means a ship registered in the United Kingdom habitually used or used at the time of the alleged offence for the purposes of carrying passengers or goods for reward.

(9) It shall be an offence to procure or attempt to procure the commission of a homosexual act between two other male persons.

PART VI

(10) From the commencement of this section a person who commits or is party to the commission of an offence under subsection (7) or subsection (9) above shall be liable on conviction on indictment to imprisonment for a term not exceeding two years or to a fine or to both and on summary conviction to imprisonment for a term not exceeding 3 months, or to a fine not exceeding the prescribed sum (within the meaning of section 289B of the 1975 Act).

(11) It shall be a defence to a charge of committing a homosexual act under subsection (7)(*c*) above that the person so charged being under the age of 24 years who had not previously been charged with like offence, had reasonable cause to believe that the other person was of or above the age of twenty-one years.

(12) A person who knowingly lives wholly or in part on the earnings of another from male prostitution or who solicits or importunes any male person for the purpose of procuring the commission of a homosexual act within the meaning of subsection (6) above shall be liable:

(*a*) on summary conviction to imprisonment for a term not exceeding six months; or

(*b*) on conviction on indictment to imprisonment for a term not exceeding two years.

(13) Premises shall be treated for the purposes of sections 13 and 14 of the Sexual Offences (Scotland) Act 1976 as a brothel if people resort to it for the purpose of homosexual acts within the meaning of subsection (6) above in circumstances in which resort thereto for heterosexual practices would have led to its being treated as a brothel for the purposes of those sections. 1976 c. 67.

(14) No proceedings for an offence to which this subsection applies shall be commenced after the expiration of twelve months from the date on which that offence was committed. This subsection applies to:

(*a*) the offences mentioned in subsections (7) and (9) above; and

(*b*) any offence under subsection (12) above which consists of soliciting or importuning any male person for the purpose of procuring the commission of a homosexual act.

81.—(1) In this Act— Interpretation etc.

" the 1975 Act " means the Criminal Procedure (Scotland) Act 1975; 1975 c. 21.

" constable " means a constable within the meaning of the Police (Scotland) Act 1967. 1967 c. 77.

PART VI

(2) Except where the context otherwise requires, expressions used in this Act and in the 1975 Act shall have the same meanings in this Act as in that Act.

Financial provisions.

82. There shall be defrayed out of money provided by Parliament any increase attributable to the provisions of this Act in the sums payable out of such money under any other Act.

Transitional provisions, consequential amendments and repeals.

83.—(1) Schedule 6 to this Act shall have effect for the purpose of the transition to the provisions of this Act from the law in force before the commencement of those provisions and with respect to the application of this Act to things done before the commencement of those provisions.

(2) The enactments specified in Schedule 7 to this Act shall have effect subject to the amendments there specified, being minor amendments or amendments consequential on the provisions of this Act.

(3) The enactments specified in Schedule 8 to this Act (which include certain spent provisions) are hereby repealed to the extent specified in the third column of that Schedule.

Short title, commencement and extent.

84.—(1) This Act may be cited as the Criminal Justice (Scotland) Act 1980.

(2) This Act shall come into force on such date as the Secretary of State may appoint by order made by statutory instrument; and different dates may be so appointed for different provisions or different purposes.

(3) Any order under subsection (2) above may make such transitional provision as appears to the Secretary of State to be expedient in connection with the provisions thereby brought into force.

(4) Subject to subsections (5) to (7) below, this Act extends to Scotland only.

(5) This section and the following provisions extend to England and Wales—

section 22;

section 51;

section 66 for the purposes of the construction mentioned in subsection (1) of that section;

paragraphs 2, so far as relating to section 22, and 8 to 10 of Schedule 6;

paragraphs 6(*a*), 7 to 12, 24, 58 and 79 of Schedule 7; and

1961 c. 39. Schedule 8 so far as relating to the Criminal Justice Act 1961 and to section 365 of the 1975 Act.

PART VI

(6) This section, section 22, section 51, section 66 for the purposes of the construction mentioned in subsection (1) of that section, paragraphs 2, so far as relating to section 22, and 8 to 10 of Schedule 6, paragraphs 6(*a*), 7 to 12 and 77 of Schedule 7, and Schedule 8 so far as relating to the Criminal Justice Act 1961 extend to Northern Ireland.

(7) This section, paragraphs 6(*a*) and 10(*a*) of Schedule 7, and Schedule 8 so far as relating to section 32(2)(*b*) of the Criminal Justice Act 1961, extend to the Channel Islands and the Isle of Man.

SCHEDULES

SCHEDULE 1

Section 26.

CERTIFICATES AS TO PROOF OF CERTAIN ROUTINE MATTERS

1 Enactment	2 Persons who may purport to sign certificate	3 Matters which may be certified
THE ROAD TRAFFIC REGULATION ACT 1967 (c. 76) The enactments specified in section 78A(3) (speeding offences generally).	Two police officers who have tested the apparatus.	The accuracy of any particular— (*a*) speedometer fitted to a police vehicle; (*b*) odometer fitted to a police vehicle; (*c*) radar meter; or (*d*) apparatus for measuring speed, time or distance, identified in the certificate by reference to its number or otherwise.
THE MISUSE OF DRUGS ACT 1971 (c. 38) Sections 4, 5, 6, 8, 9, 12, 13, 19 and 20 (various offences concerning controlled drugs).	Two analysts who have analysed the substance and each of whom is either a person possessing the qualifications (qualifying persons for appointment as public analysts) prescribed by regulations made under section 89 of the Food and Drugs Act 1955 (c. 16), or section 27 of the Food and Drugs (Scotland) Act 1956 (c. 30), or a person authorised by the Secretary of State to make analyses for the purposes of the provisions of the Misuse of Drugs Act 1971 mentioned in column 1.	The type and classification of any particular substance, identified in the certificate by reference to a label or otherwise, which is alleged to be a controlled drug within the meaning of section 2 of the Act referred to in column 1.
THE IMMIGRATION ACT 1971 (c. 77) Section 24(1)(*a*) in so far as it relates to entry in breach of a deportation order, section 24(1)(*b*) and section 26(1)(*f*) in so far as it relates to a requirement of regulations	An officer authorised to do so by the Secretary of State.	In relation to a person identified in the certificate— (*a*) the date, place or means of his arrival in, or any removal of him from, the United Kingdom;

1 Enactment	2 Persons who may purport to sign certificate	3 Matters which may be certified
The Immigration Act 1971 (c. 77)—*cont.* (various offences concerning persons entering, or remaining in, the United Kingdom).		(*b*) any limitation on, or condition attached to, any leave for him to enter or remain in the United Kingdom; (*c*) the date and method of service of any notice of, or of variation of conditions attached to, such leave.
The Social Security Act 1975 (c. 14) Section 146(3)(*c*) (false statements etc. to obtain payments).	An officer authorised to do so by the Secretary of State.	In relation to a person identified in the certificate— (*a*) the assessment, award, or nature of any benefit applied for by him; (*b*) the transmission or handing over of any payment to him.
The Child Benefit Act 1975 (c. 61) Section 11 (false statements etc. to obtain child benefit).	An officer authorised to do so by the Secretary of State.	In relation to a person identified in the certificate— (*a*) the assessment, award, or nature of any benefit applied for by him; (*b*) the transmission or handing over of any payment to him.
The Supplementary Benefits Act 1976 (c. 71) Section 21 (false statements).	An officer authorised to do so by the Secretary of State.	In relation to a person identified in the certificate— (*a*) the assessment, award, or nature of any benefit applied for by him; (*b*) the transmission or handing over of any payment to him.

Section 33.

SCHEDULE 2

SOLEMN APPEALS

In the 1975 Act—

1. For section 228 (right of appeal), there shall be substituted the following section—

"Right of Appeal.

228.—(1) Any person convicted on indictment may appeal in accordance with the provisions of this Part of this Act, to the High Court—

(*a*) against such conviction;

(*b*) against the sentence passed on such conviction; or

(*c*) against both such conviction and such sentence:

Provided that there shall be no appeal against any sentence fixed by law.

(2) By an appeal under subsection (1) of this section, a person may bring under review of the High Court any alleged miscarriage of justice in the proceedings in which he was convicted, including any alleged miscarriage of justice on the basis of the existence and significance of additional evidence which was not heard at the trial and which was not available and could not reasonably have been made available at the trial.".

2. Section 229 (certificate by judge that case appealable) shall cease to have effect.

3. For section 231 (time for appealing), there shall be substituted the following section—

"Intimation of intention to appeal.

231.—(1) Subject to section 236B(2) of this Act, where a person desires to appeal under section 228(1)(*a*) or (*c*) of this Act, he shall, within two weeks of the final determination of the proceedings, lodge with the Clerk of Justiciary written intimation of intention to appeal and send a copy to the Crown Agent.

(2) Such intimation shall identify the proceedings and be in as nearly as may be the form prescribed by Act of Adjournal under this Act.

(3) On such intimation being lodged by a person in custody, the Clerk of Justiciary shall give notice thereof to the Secretary of State.

(4) For the purposes of subsection (1) above and section 270(2) of this Act, proceedings shall be deemed finally determined on the day on which sentence is passed in open court; except that, where in relation to an appeal under section 228(1)(*a*) of this Act sentence is deferred under section 219 of this Act, they shall be deemed finally determined on the day on which sentence is first so deferred in open court.".

4. Section 232 (calculating days of appeal etc.) shall cease to have effect.

5. For section 233 (forms of appeal) there shall be substituted the following section—

"Note of appeal.

233.—(1) Subject to section 236B(2) of this Act, within six weeks of lodging intimation of intention to appeal or, in the case of an appeal against sentence alone, within two weeks of the passing of the sentence in open court, the convicted person may lodge a written note of appeal with the Clerk of Justiciary who shall send a copy to the judge who presided at the trial and to the Crown Agent: Provided that the first mentioned period may be extended, before expiry thereof, by the Clerk of Justiciary.

(2) Such a note shall identify the proceedings, contain a full statement of all the grounds of appeal and be in as nearly as may be the form prescribed by Act of Adjournal under this Act.

(3) Except by leave of the High Court on cause shown it shall not be competent for an appellant to found any aspect of his appeal on a ground not contained in the note of appeal.

(4) On a note of appeal against sentence alone being lodged by an appellant in custody the Clerk of Justiciary shall give notice thereof to the Secretary of State.".

6. In section 234 (presentation of appeal in writing), in each of subsections (1) and (3) the words "or an applicant for leave to appeal" and "or application for leave to appeal" shall cease to have effect.

7. In section 236 (proceedings in sheriff court to be furnished) the words "or application for leave to appeal" shall cease to have effect.

8. After section 236 there shall be inserted the following sections—

"Judge's report.

236A.—(1) As soon as is reasonably practicable after his receipt of the copy note of appeal sent to him under section 233(1) of this Act, the judge who presided at the trial shall furnish the Clerk of Justiciary with a report in writing giving the judge's opinion on the case generally and on the grounds contained in the note of appeal; and the Clerk of Justiciary shall send a copy of the report to the convicted person or his solicitor, to the Crown Agent, and, in a case referred under section 263(1) of this Act, to the Secretary of State.

(2) Where the judge's report is not furnished as mentioned in subsection (1) above, the High Court may call for such report to be furnished within such period as it may specify or, if it thinks fit, hear and determine the appeal without such report.

(3) Subject to subsection (1) above, the report of the judge shall be available only to the High Court and the parties.

Computation of periods

236B.—(1) Where the last day of any period mentioned in sections 231(1) and 233(1) of this Act falls on a day which the office of the Clerk of Justiciary is

SCH. 2

closed, such period shall extend to and include the next day on which such office is open.

(2) Any period mentioned in section 231(1) or 233(1) of this Act may be extended at any time by the High Court in respect of any convicted person; and application for such extension may be made under this subsection and shall be in as nearly as may be the form prescribed by Act of Adjournal under this Act.

Signing of documents.

236C. Any intimation of intention to appeal, note of appeal or application in terms of section 236B(2) of this Act shall be signed by the convicted person or by his counsel or solicitor.".

9. For section 237 (judge's notes and report to be furnished), there shall be substituted the following section—

"Note of Proceedings.

237. The High Court where hearing an appeal under this Part of this Act may require the judge who presided at the trial to produce any notes taken by him of the proceedings at the trial.".

10. In section 238 (admission of appellant to bail)—

(*a*) in subsection (2), after the words "determine it or" there shall be inserted the words "without prejudice to section 3 of the Bail etc. (Scotland) Act 1980"; and

(*b*) after subsection (2) there shall be inserted the following subsection—

"(3) For the purposes of subsections (1) and (2) above, 'appellant' includes not only a person who has lodged a note of appeal but also one who has lodged an intimation of intention to appeal.".

11. In section 239(1) (clerk to give notice of date of hearing), for the words from "for leave to appeal or" to "by the court" there shall be substituted the words "under section 236B(2) of this Act".

12. In section 240 (appellant may be present at hearing), the words "and on an application for leave to appeal" shall cease to have effect.

13. For section 244 (abandonment of appeal), there shall be substituted the following section—

"Abandonment of appeal.

244.—(1) An appellant may abandon his appeal by lodging with the Clerk of Justiciary a notice of abandonment in as nearly as may be the form prescribed by Act of Adjournal under this Act; and on such notice being lodged the appeal shall be deemed to have been dismissed by the court.

(2) A person who has appealed against both conviction and sentence may abandon the appeal in so far as it is against conviction and may proceed with it against sentence alone.".

Sch. 2

14. In section 245(3) (quorum and sitting of High Court) the words "from the sheriff court" shall cease to have effect.

15. In section 247 (powers which may be exercised by a single judge)—

(a) the words "to give leave to appeal", shall cease to have effect;

(b) for the words "notice of appeal", there shall be substituted the words "intimation of intention to appeal and note of appeal"; and

(c) the words "or of an application for leave to appeal" shall cease to have effect.

16. For section 252 (supplemental powers of High Court), there shall be substituted the following section—

"Powers of High Court. 252. Without prejudice to any existing power of the High Court, that court may for the purposes of an appeal under section 228(1) of this Act—

(a) order the production of any document or other thing connected with the proceedings;

(b) hear any additional evidence relevant to any alleged miscarriage of justice or order such evidence to be heard by a judge of the High Court or by such other person as it may appoint for that purpose;

(c) take account of any circumstances relevant to the case which were not before the trial judge;

(d) remit to any fit person to enquire and report in regard to any matter or circumstance affecting the appeal;

(e) appoint a person with expert knowledge to act as assessor to the High Court in any case where it appears to the court that such expert knowledge is required for the proper determination of the case.".

17. Section 253(2) (evidence on commission) shall cease to have effect.

18. For section 254 (determination of appeals) there shall be substituted the following section—

"Disposal of appeals. 254.—(1) The High Court may, subject to subsection (4) below, dispose of an appeal against conviction by—

(a) affirming the verdict of the trial court;

(b) setting aside the verdict of the trial court and either quashing the conviction or substituting therefor an amended verdict of guilty:

Provided that an amended verdict of guilty must be one which could have been returned on the indictment before the trial court; or

SCH. 2

(*c*) setting aside the verdict of the trial court and granting authority to bring a new prosecution in accordance with section 255 of this Act.

(2) In setting aside, under subsection (1) above, a verdict the High Court may quash any sentence imposed on the appellant as respects the indictment, and—

(*a*) in a case where it substitutes an amended verdict of guilty, whether or not the sentence related to the verdict set aside ; or

(*b*) in any other case, where the sentence did not so relate,

may pass another (but not more severe) sentence in substitution for the sentence so quashed.

(3) The High Court may, subject to subsection (4) below, dispose of an appeal against sentence by—

(*a*) affirming such sentence ; or

(*b*) if the Court thinks that, having regard to all the circumstances, including any additional evidence such as is mentioned in section 228(2) of this Act, a different sentence should have been passed, quashing the sentence and passing another sentence whether more or less severe in substitution therefor.

(4) In relation to any appeal under section 228(1) of this Act, the High Court shall, where it appears to it that the appellant committed the act charged against him but that he was insane when he did so, dispose of the appeal by—

(*a*) setting aside the verdict of the trial court and substituting therefor a verdict of acquittal on the ground of insanity ; and

(*b*) quashing any sentence imposed on the appellant as respects the indictment and ordering that he be detained in a state hospital or such other hospital as for special reasons the court may specify.

(5) The provisions of subsection (4) of section 174 of this Act shall apply to an order under subsection (4)(*b*) above as they apply to an order under that section.".

19. For section 255 (substitution of verdict) there shall be substituted the following section—

"Supplementary provisions where High Court authorises new prosecution.

255.—(1) Where authority is granted under section 254(1)(*c*) of this Act, a new prosecution may be brought charging the accused with the same or any similar offence arising out of the same facts ; and the proceedings out of which the appeal arose shall not be a bar to such new prosecution:

Provided that no sentence may be passed on conviction under the new prosecution which could not have been passed on conviction under the earlier proceedings.

Sch. 2

(2) A new prosecution may be brought under this section, notwithstanding that any time limit (other than the time limit mentioned in subsection (3) below), for the commencement of such proceedings has elapsed.

(3) Proceedings in a prosecution under this section shall be commenced within two months of the date on which authority to bring the prosecution was granted; and for the purposes of this subsection proceedings shall, in a case where such warrant is executed without unreasonable delay, be deemed to be commenced on the date on which a warrant to apprehend or to cite the accused is granted, and shall in any other case be deemed to be commenced on the date on which the warrant is executed.

(4) Where the two months mentioned in subsection (3) above elapse and no new prosecution has been brought under this section, the order under section 254(1)(*c*) of this Act setting aside the verdict shall have the effect, for all purposes, of an acquittal.".

20. In section 256 (frivolous appeals) for the word " notice " there shall be substituted the word " note ".

21. In section 257 (failure to appear at hearing), the words " or applicant " and, in both places where they occur, the words " or application for leave to appeal " shall cease to have effect.

22. In section 263(1) (prerogative of mercy)—

(*a*) the words " or an application for leave to appeal " shall cease to have effect; and

(*b*) for the words from " either " to the end there shall be substituted the words " refer the whole case to the High Court and the case shall be heard and determined, subject to any directions the High Court may make, as if it were an appeal under this Part of this Act.".

23. In Section 264 (disqualification, forfeiture etc.), in each of subsections (1) and (2) for the words " ten days ", " a note of appeal or of application for leave to appeal " and " the determination thereof " there shall be substituted, respectively, the words " two weeks ", " an intimation of intention to appeal (or in the case of an appeal under section 228(1)(*b*) of this Act a note of appeal) " and " such appeal, if it is proceeded with, is determined ".

24. In section 265 (fines and caution)—

(*a*) in subsection (3) the words " either upon grounds of law alone, or with the certificate of the said judge upon any grounds mentioned in section 228(*b*) of this Act," shall cease to have effect; and

(*b*) in subsection (5), for the words from " a note " to " days " there shall be substituted the words " an intimation of intention to appeal within two weeks ".

SCH. 2

25. In section 269 (extract convictions) for the words " ten days ", " a note of appeal or of application for leave to appeal ", and " the determination thereof " there shall be substituted, respectively, the words " two weeks ", " an intimation of intention to appeal (or in the case of an appeal under section 228(1)(*b*) of this Act a note of appeal) " and " such appeal, if it is proceeded with, is determined ".

26. In section 270 (custody of trial documents etc.)—

(*a*) in subsection (2)—

(i) for the words " ten days ", in both places where they occur, there shall be substituted the words " two weeks " ;

(ii) for the words " actual day on which the conviction took place " there shall be substituted the words " final determination (as construed in accordance with section 231(4) of this Act) of the proceedings " ;

(iii) for the words " a note of appeal or application for leave to appeal " there shall be substituted the words " an intimation of intention to appeal (or in the case of an appeal under section 228(1)(*b*) of this Act a note of appeal) " ;

(iv) for the words " a note of appeal or of application for leave to appeal has been lodged " there shall be substituted the words " there has been such lodgement " ; and

(v) for the words " determination thereof " there shall be substituted the words " appeal, if it is proceeded with, is determined " ;

(*b*) in subsection (3), for the words " an appellant or applicant who has lodged a note of appeal or of application for leave to appeal " there shall be substituted the words " a person who has lodged an intimation of intention to appeal (or in the case of an appeal under section 228(1)(*b*) of this Act a note of appeal) " ; and

(*c*) in subsection (4)—

(i) for the words " note of appeal or application for leave to appeal " there shall be substituted the words " intimation of intention to appeal (or, in the case of an appeal under section 228(1)(*b*) of this Act, note of appeal) " ;

(ii) for the words " ten days " there shall be substituted the words " two weeks " ; and

(iii) at the end there shall be added the words " ; and they shall be so dealt with if, there having been such intimation, the appeal is not proceeded with.".

27. In section 271 (Clerk of Justiciary to furnish forms etc.) for the words " notices of appeal " there shall be substituted the words " intimations of intention to appeal, notes of appeal ".

28. In section 272 (note to be kept of appeal) the words " or of application for leave to appeal ", the words " or application for leave

to appeal " in the three places where they occur, and the words " or application " in the fourth place where they occur, shall cease to have effect. SCH. 2

29. In section 273(1) (register of appeals) for the words " a note of appeal or note of application for leave to " there shall be substituted the words " intimation of intention to appeal or, in the case of an appeal under section 228(1)(*b*) of this Act, note of ".

30. In section 274(1) (shorthand notes of trial) the words " or may be authorised " and " or application for leave to appeal " shall cease to have effect.

31. In section 277 (non-compliance with certain provisions)—

(*a*) in subsection (1), the words " and applications for leave to appeal ", and the words " or application " in both places where they occur, shall cease to have effect;

(*b*) in subsection (2), the words " section 229 ", " section 232 " and " section 233 " shall cease to have effect; and

(*c*) in subsection (2), the words " section 236B " and " section 236C " shall be added at the appropriate places to the provisions mentioned in the subsection.

32. In section 280 (appeals against hospital orders etc.) for the words " a conviction " there shall be substituted the word " sentence ".

SCHEDULE 3

Section 34.

SUMMARY APPEALS

In the 1975 Act—

1. For section 442 (appeal by stated case), there shall be substituted the following sections—

" Right of appeal.

442.—(1) Without prejudice to any right of appeal under section 453A of this Act—

(*a*) any person convicted in summary proceedings may appeal under this section to the High Court—

(i) against such conviction;

(ii) against the sentence passed on such conviction; or

(iii) against both such conviction and such sentence;

(*b*) the prosecutor in such proceedings may so appeal on a point of law—

(i) against an acquittal in such proceedings; or

(ii) against a sentence passed in such proceedings.

Sch. 3

(2) By an appeal under subsection (1)(*a*) of this section or, as the case may be, against acquittal under subsection (1)(*b*) of this section, an appellant may bring under review of the High Court any alleged miscarriage of justice in the proceedings, including, in the case of an appeal under the said subsection (1)(*a*), any alleged miscarriage of justice on the basis of the existence and significance of additional evidence which was not heard at the trial and which was not available and could not reasonably have been made available at the trial.

Method of appeal against conviction or conviction and sentence.

442A.—(1) Where a person desires to appeal under section 442(1)(*a*)(i) or (iii) or (*b*) of this Act, he shall pursue such appeal in accordance with the provisions of sections 444 to 453, 453D and 453E of this Act.

(2) A person who has appealed against both conviction and sentence, may abandon the appeal in so far as it is against conviction and may proceed with it against sentence alone, subject to such procedure as may be prescribed by Act of Adjournal under this Act.

Method of appeal against sentence alone.

442B. Where a person desires to appeal against sentence alone, under section 442(1)(*a*)(ii) of this Act, he shall pursue such appeal in accordance with the provisions of sections 453B to 453E of this Act:

Provided that nothing in this section shall prevent a convicted person from proceeding by way of a bill of suspension in respect of any alleged fundamental irregularity relating to the imposition of the sentence.".

2. In section 443 (appeals against hospital orders etc.), for the words " a conviction " there shall be substituted the word " sentence ".

3. In section 444 (manner and time of appeal)—

(*a*) for subsection (1) there shall be substituted the following subsections—

" (1) An appeal under section 442(1)(*a*)(i) or (iii) or (*b*) of this Act shall be by application for a stated case, which application shall—

(*a*) be made within one week of the final determination of the proceedings ;

(*b*) contain a full statement of all the matters which the appellant desires to bring under review and where the appeal is also against sentence, a statement of that fact ; and

(*c*) be signed by the appellant or his solicitor and lodged with the clerk of court ;

and a copy of the application shall within the period mentioned in paragraph (*a*) above be sent by the appellant to the respondent or the respondent's solicitor.

(1A) The clerk of the court shall enter in the record of the proceedings the date when an application under subsection (1) above was lodged.

(1B) The appellant may, at any time within the period of three weeks mentioned in subsection (1) of section 448 of this Act, or within any further period afforded him by virtue of subsection (6) of that section, amend any matter stated in his application or add a new matter; and he shall intimate any such amendment, or addition, to the respondent or the respondent's solicitor."; and

(*b*) in subsection (5), after the word "under" there shall be inserted the words "subsection (3) of".

4. Section 445 (caution by appellant) shall cease to have effect.

5. In section 446 (procedure where appellant in custody), for subsection (1) there shall be substituted the following subsection—

"(1) If an appellant under section 444 of this Act is in custody, the court may—

(*a*) grant bail;

(*b*) grant a sist of execution;

(*c*) make any other interim order.".

6. For subsection (1) of section 447 (draft stated case to be prepared), there shall be substituted the following subsection—

"(1) Within three weeks of the final determination of proceedings in respect of which an application for a stated case is made under section 444 of this Act—

(*a*) where the appeal is taken from the district court and the trial was presided over by a justice of the peace or justices of the peace, the justice, or justices, with such assistance from the clerk of court as may be required; or

(*b*) in any other case the judge who presided at the trial,

shall prepare a draft stated case, and the clerk of the court concerned shall forthwith issue the draft to the appellant or his solicitor and a duplicate thereof to the respondent or his solicitor.".

7. In section 448 (adjustment and signature of case)—

(*a*) for subsections (1) and (2) there shall be substituted the following subsections—

"(1) Subject to subsection (6) below, within three weeks of the issue of the draft stated case under section 447 of this Act, each party shall cause to be transmitted to the court and to the other parties or their solicitors a note of any adjustments he proposes be made to the draft case or shall intimate that he has no such proposal:

Provided that adjustments proposed shall relate to evidence heard (or purported to have been heard) at the

SCH. 3

trial and not to such additional evidence as is mentioned in section 442(2) of this Act.

(2) Subject to subsection (6) below, if the period mentioned in subsection (1) above has expired and the appellant has not lodged adjustments and has failed to intimate that he has no adjustments to propose, he shall be deemed to have abandoned his appeal; and subsection (4) of section 446 of this Act shall apply accordingly.

(2A) If adjustments are proposed under subsection (1) above or if the judge desires to make any alterations to the draft case there shall, within one week of the expiry of the period mentioned in that subsection or as the case may be of any further period afforded under subsection (6) below, be a hearing (unless the appellant has, or has been deemed to have, abandoned his appeal) for the purpose of considering such adjustments or alterations.

(2B) Where a party neither attends nor secures that he is represented at a hearing under subsection (2A) above, the hearing shall nevertheless proceed.

(2C) Where at a hearing under subsection (2A) above—

(*a*) any adjustment proposed under subsection (1) above by a party (and not withdrawn) is rejected by the judge; or

(*b*) any alteration to the draft case proposed by the judge is not accepted by all the parties,

that fact shall be recorded in the minute of the proceedings of the hearing.

(2D) Within two weeks of the date of the hearing under subsection (2A) above or, where there is no hearing, within two weeks of the expiry of the period mentioned in subsection (1) above, the judge shall (unless the appellant has been deemed to have abandoned the appeal) state and sign the case and shall append to the case—

(*a*) any adjustment, proposed under subsection (1) above, which is rejected by him, a note of any evidence rejected by him which is alleged to support that adjustment and the reasons for his rejection of that adjustment and evidence; and

(*b*) a note of the evidence upon which he bases any finding of fact challenged, on the basis that it is unsupported by the evidence, by a party at the hearing under subsection (2A) above.";

(*b*) for subsections (3) to (5) there shall be substituted the following subsections—

"(3) As soon as the case is signed under subsection (2D) above the clerk of court—

(*a*) shall send the case to the appellant or his solicitor and a duplicate thereof to the respondent or his solicitor; and

Sch. 3

(*b*) shall transmit the complaint, productions and any other proceedings in the cause to the Clerk of Justiciary.

(4) Subject to subsection (6) below, within one week of receiving the case the appellant or his solicitor, as the case may be, shall cause it to be lodged with the Clerk of Justiciary.

(5) Subject to subsection (6) below, if the appellant or his solicitor fails to comply with subsection (4) above the appellant shall be deemed to have abandoned the appeal; and subsection (4) of section 446 of this Act shall apply accordingly." ;

(*c*) in subsection (6), after the word " subsection " there shall be inserted the words " (1) or " ; and

(*d*) in subsection (8), after the word " under " there shall be inserted the words " subsection (6) of ".

8. In section 449 (abandonment of appeal)—

(*a*) in subsection (1)—

(i) for the words " under section 442 ", there shall be substituted the words " in an appeal such as is mentioned in section 444(1) " ; and

(ii) after the word " respondent " there shall be inserted the words " or the respondent's solicitor " ; and

(*b*) in subsection (2) at the beginning there shall be inserted the words " Subject to section 453A of this Act, ".

9. In section 450 (record of procedure on appeal), for the words " being taken under section 442 of this Act " there shall be substituted the words " such as is mentioned in section 444(1) of this Act being taken ".

10. For section 451 (computation of time), there shall be substituted the following section—

" Computation of time.

451.—(1) If any period of time specified in any provision of this Part of this Act relating to appeals expires on a Saturday, Sunday or court holiday prescribed for the relevant court, the period shall be extended to expire on the next day which is not a Saturday, Sunday or such court holiday.

(2) Where a judge against whose judgment an appeal is taken is temporarily absent from duty for any cause, the sheriff principal of the sheriffdom in which the court at which the judgment was pronounced is situated may extend any period specified in sections 447(1) and 448(2A) and (2D) of this Act for such period as he considers reasonable.

(3) For the purposes of sections 444(1)(*a*) and 447(1) of this Act, summary proceedings shall be deemed to be

SCH. 3

finally determined on the day on which sentence is passed in open court; except that, where in relation to an appeal under section 442(1)(*a*)(i) or (*b*)(i) of this Act sentence is deferred under section 432 of this Act, they shall be deemed finally determined on the day on which sentence is first so deferred in open court.".

11. For section 452 (hearing of appeal), there shall be substituted the following sections—

"Hearing of appeal.

452.—(1) A stated case under this Part of this Act shall be heard by the High Court on such date as it may fix.

(2) For the avoidance of doubt, where an appellant, in his application under section 444(1) of this Act (or in a duly made amendment or addition to that application), refers to an alleged miscarriage of justice, but in stating a case under section 448(2D) of this Act the inferior court is unable to take the allegation into account, the High Court may nevertheless have regard to the allegation at a hearing under subsection (1) above.

(3) Except by leave of the High Court on cause shown, it shall not be competent for an appellant to found any aspect of his appeal on a matter not contained in his application under section 444(1) of this Act (or in a duly made amendment or addition to that application).

(4) Without prejudice to any existing power of the High Court, that court may in hearing a stated case—

(*a*) order the production of any document or other thing connected with the proceedings;

(*b*) hear any additional evidence relevant to any alleged miscarriage of justice or order such evidence to be heard by a judge of the High Court or by such other person as it may appoint for that purpose;

(*c*) take account of any circumstances relevant to the case which were not before the trial judge;

(*d*) remit to any fit person to enquire and report in regard to any matter or circumstance affecting the appeal;

(*e*) appoint a person with expert knowledge to act as assessor to the High Court in any case where it appears to the court that such expert knowledge is required for the proper determination of the case;

(*f*) take account of any matter proposed in any adjustment rejected by the trial judge and of the reasons for such rejection;

(*g*) take account of any evidence contained in a note of evidence such as is mentioned in section 448(2D) of this Act.

SCH. 3

(5) The High Court may at the hearing remit the stated case back to the inferior court to be amended and returned.

Disposal of stated case appeal.

452A.—(1) The High Court may, subject to section 453D(1) of this Act, dispose of a stated case by—

(*a*) remitting the cause to the inferior court with their opinion and any direction thereon;

(*b*) affirming the verdict of the inferior court;

(*c*) setting aside the verdict of the inferior court and either quashing the conviction or substituting therefor an amended verdict of guilty:

Provided that an amended verdict of guilty must be one which could have been returned on the complaint before the inferior court; or

(*d*) setting aside the verdict of the inferior court and granting authority to bring a new prosecution in accordance with section 452B of this Act.

(2) In an appeal against both conviction and sentence the High Court shall, subject to section 453D(1) of this Act, dispose of the appeal against sentence by exercise of the power mentioned in section 453C(1) of this Act.

(3) In setting aside, under subsection (1) above, a verdict the High Court may quash any sentence imposed on the appellant as respects the complaint, and—

(*a*) in a case where it substitutes an amended verdict of guilty, whether or not the sentence related to the verdict set aside; or

(*b*) in any other case, where the sentence did not so relate,

may pass another (but not more severe) sentence in substitution for the sentence so quashed.

(4) Where an appeal against acquittal is sustained, the High Court may—

(*a*) convict and sentence the respondent;

(*b*) remit the case to the inferior court with instructions to convict and sentence the respondent, who shall be bound to attend any diet fixed by the inferior court for such purpose; or

(*c*) remit the case to the inferior court with their opinion thereon:

Provided that the High Court shall not in any case increase the sentence beyond the maximum sentence which could have been passed by the inferior court.

(5) The High Court shall have power in an appeal under this Part of this Act to award such expenses both in the High Court and in the inferior court as it may think fit.

D

Sch. 3

(6) Where, following an appeal (other than an appeal under section 442(1)(*a*)(ii) or 442(1)(*b*) of this Act), the appellant remains liable to imprisonment or detention under the sentence of the inferior court, or is so liable under a sentence passed in the appeal proceedings the High Court shall have power where at the time of disposal of the appeal the appellant—

(*a*) was at liberty on bail, to grant warrant to apprehend and imprison (or detain) the appellant for a term, to run from the date of such apprehension, not longer than that part of the term or terms of imprisonment (or detention) specified in the sentence brought under review which remained unexpired at the date of liberation;

(*b*) is serving a term or terms of imprisonment (or detention) imposed in relation to a conviction subsequent to the conviction appealed against, to exercise the like powers in regard to him as may be exercised, in relation to an appeal which has been abandoned, by a court of summary jurisdiction in pursuance of section 446(5) of this Act.

Supplementary provisions where High Court authorises new prosecution.

452B.—(1) Where authority is granted under section 452A(1)(*d*) of this Act, a new prosecution may be brought charging the accused with the same or any similar offence arising out of the same facts; and the proceedings out of which the stated case arose shall not be a bar to such prosecution:

Provided that no sentence may be passed on conviction under the new prosecution which could not have been passed on conviction under the earlier proceedings.

(2) A new prosecution may be brought under this section, notwithstanding that any time limit (other than the time limit mentioned in subsection (3) below) for the commencement of such proceedings has elapsed.

(3) Proceedings in a prosecution under this section shall be commenced within two months of the date on which authority to bring the prosecution was granted; and for the purposes of this subsection proceedings shall, in a case where such warrant is executed without unreasonable delay, be deemed to be commenced on the date on which a warrant to apprehend or to cite the accused is granted, and shall in any other case be deemed to be commenced on the date on which the warrant is executed.

(4) Where the two months mentioned in subsection (3) above elapse and no new prosecution has been brought under this section, the order under section 452A(1)(*d*) of this Act setting aside the verdict shall have the effect, for all purposes, of an acquittal.".

Sch. 3

12. In section 453 (consent by prosecutor to set aside conviction)—

(*a*) in subsection (1) for the words " section 442 " there shall be substituted the words " section 442(1)(*a*)(i) or (iii) " ;

(*b*) in subsection (2) after the word " appellant " where it first occurs there shall be inserted the words " or his solicitor " ;

(*c*) in each of paragraphs (*a*) and (*b*) of subsection (5), for the words " 10 days " there shall be substituted the words " 2 weeks ".

13. After section 453 of the 1975 Act there shall be inserted the following sections—

" Appeal by bill of suspension or advocation on ground of miscarriage of justice.

453A.—(1) Notwithstanding section 449(2) of this Act, a party to a summary prosecution may, where an appeal under section 442 of this Act would be incompetent or would in the circumstances be inappropriate, appeal to the High Court, by bill of suspension against a conviction, or as the case may be by advocation against an acquittal, on the ground of an alleged miscarriage of justice in the proceedings:

Provided that where the alleged miscarriage of justice is referred to in an application, under section 444(1) of this Act, for a stated case as regards the proceedings (or in a duly made amendment or addition to that application) an appeal under subsection (1) above shall not proceed without the leave of the High Court until the appeal to which the application relates has been finally disposed of or abandoned.

(2) Sections 452(4)(*a*) to (*e*), 452A(1)(*d*), 452A(3) and 452B of this Act shall apply to appeals under this section as they apply to appeals such as are mentioned in section 444(1) of this Act.

(3) The foregoing provisions of this section shall be without prejudice to any rule of law relating to bills of suspension or advocation in so far as such rule of law is not inconsistent with those provisions.

Appeals against sentence only.

453B.—(1) An appeal under section 442(1)(*a*)(ii) of this Act shall be by note of appeal, which shall state the ground of appeal.

(2) The note of appeal shall, within one week of the passing of the sentence, be lodged with the clerk of the court from which the appeal is to be taken.

(3) The clerk of court on receipt of the note of appeal shall—

(*a*) send a copy of the note to the respondent or his solicitor ; and

(*b*) obtain a report from the judge who sentenced the convicted person.

SCH. 3

(4) The clerk of court shall within two weeks of the passing of the sentence against which the appeal is taken—

(*a*) send to the Clerk of Justiciary the note of appeal, together with the report mentioned in subsection (3)(*b*) above, a certified copy of the complaint, the minute of proceedings and any other relevant documents; and

(*b*) send copies of that report to the appellant and respondent or their solicitors:

Provided that the sheriff principal of the sheriffdom in which the judgment was pronounced may, where a judge is temporarily absent from duty for any cause, extend the period of two weeks specified in this subsection for such period as the sheriff principal considers reasonable.

(5) Where the judge's report is not furnished within the period mentioned in subsection (4) above, the High Court may extend such period or, if it thinks fit, hear and determine the appeal without such report.

(6) Subsections (3), (4) and (5) of section 444 of this Act shall apply where an appellant fails to comply with the requirement of subsection (2) above as they apply where an applicant fails to comply with any of the requirements of subsection (1) of that section.

(7) An appellant under section 442(1)(*a*)(ii) of this Act may at any time prior to the hearing of the appeal abandon his appeal by minute, signed by himself or his solicitor, lodged—

(*a*) in a case where the note of appeal has not yet been sent under subsection (4)(*a*) above to the Clerk of Justiciary, with the clerk of court;

(*b*) in any other case, with the Clerk of Justiciary,

and intimated to the respondent.

(8) Sections 446, 450 and 452(4)(*a*) to (*e*) of this Act shall apply to appeals under section 442(1)(*a*)(ii) of this Act as they apply to appeals under section 442(1)(*a*)(i) or (iii) of this Act.

Disposal of appeal by note of appeal.

453C.—(1) An appeal against sentence by note of appeal shall be heard by the High Court on such date as it may fix, and the High Court may, subject to section 453D(1) of this Act, dispose of such appeal by—

(*a*) affirming the sentence; or

(*b*) if the Court thinks that, having regard to all the circumstances, including any additional evidence such as is mentioned in section 442(2) of this Act, a different sentence should have been passed, quashing the sentence and passing another sentence, whether more or less severe, in substitution therefor:

SCH. 3

Provided that the Court shall not in any case increase the sentence beyond the maximum sentence which could have been passed by the inferior court.

(2) The High Court shall have power in an appeal by note of appeal to award such expenses both in the High Court and in the inferior court as it may think fit.

(3) Where, following an appeal under section 442(1)(*a*)(ii) of this Act, the appellant remains liable to imprisonment or detention under the sentence of the inferior court or is so liable under a sentence passed in the appeal proceedings, the High Court shall have power where at the time of disposal of the appeal the appellant—

(*a*) was at liberty on bail, to grant warrant to apprehend and imprison (or detain) the appellant for a term, to run from the date of such apprehension, not longer than that part of the term or terms of imprisonment (or detention) specified in the sentence brought under review which remained unexpired at the date of liberation ; or

(*b*) is serving a term or terms of imprisonment (or detention) imposed in relation to a conviction subsequent to the conviction in respect of which the sentence appealed against was imposed, to exercise the like powers in regard to him as may be exercised, in relation to an appeal which has been abandoned, by a court of summary jurisdiction in pursuance of section 446(5) of this Act.

Disposal of appeal where appellant insane.

453D.—(1) In relation to any appeal under section 442(1)(*a*) of this Act, the High Court shall, where it appears to it that the appellant committed the act charged against him but that he was insane when he did so, dispose of the appeal by—

(*a*) setting aside the verdict of the inferior court and substituting therefor a verdict of acquittal on the ground of insanity ; and

(*b*) quashing any sentence imposed on the appellant as respects the complaint and ordering that he be detained in a state hospital or such other hospital as for special reasons the court may specify.

(2) The provisions of subsection (4) of section 174 of this Act shall apply to an order under subsection (1)(*b*) above as they apply to an order under that section.

Failure of appellant who has been granted bail to appear personally.

453E. Where an appellant has been granted bail, whether his appeal is under this Part of this Act or otherwise, he shall appear personally in court at the diet appointed for the hearing of the appeal. If he does not appear the High Court shall either—

SCH. 3

(*a*) dispose of the appeal as if it had been abandoned (in which case subsection (4) of section 446 of this Act shall apply accordingly); or

(*b*) on cause shown permit the appeal to be heard in his absence.".

14. Section 454(2) (which provides in relation to summary proceedings that no conviction or sentence etc. shall be quashed except on certain specified grounds) shall cease to have effect.

Section 12.

SCHEDULE 4

Abolition of Mandatory First Diet

In the 1975 Act—

1. In section 68(3) (notice of previous convictions)—

(*a*) the words "where the accused pleads not guilty at the first diet" shall cease to have effect;

(*b*) for the words "second diet" in each of the three places where they occur, there shall be substituted the words "trial diet"; and

(*c*) for the words "the first diet", in the second place where they occur, there shall be substituted the words "any diet".

2. In section 69 (warrants for citation) for the words "second diet" there shall be substituted the words "trial diet".

3. In section 74 (proceedings against bodies corporate)—

(*a*) subsection (3) shall cease to have effect; and

(*b*) in subsection (4), for the words "second diet" there shall be substituted the words "trial diet".

4. For section 75 there shall be substituted the following section—

"Notice of trial diet.

75. Except where the indictment is served under section 102(1) of this Act, the notice served on the accused with the indictment shall call upon him to appear and answer to such indictment at a trial diet (either in the High Court or in the sheriff court) not less than 29 clear days after the service of such indictment and notice.".

5. For section 76 (notice for first diet) there shall be substituted the following sections—

"Preliminary diet.

76.—(1) Subject to section 20B(2) of this Act and to subsections (4) and (5) below, where a party within the appropriate period gives written notice to the court before which the trial is to take place and to the other parties—

(*a*) that he intends to raise a matter relating to the competency or relevancy of the indictment or to raise an objection such as is mentioned in section 108(1) of this Act, the court shall order that there be a diet before the trial diet;

(*b*) that he intends to submit a plea in bar of trial or to apply for separation or conjunction of charges or trials or to make an application under section 151(2) of this Act, the court may make such order as is mentioned in paragraph (*a*) above; SCH. 4

(*c*) that there is some point, as regards any matter not mentioned in paragraph (*a*) or (*b*) above, which could in his opinion be resolved with advantage before the trial and that he therefore applies for a diet to be held before the trial diet, the court may make such order as is mentioned in paragraph (*a*) above.

A party giving notice under this subsection shall specify in the notice the matter (or, as the case may be, the grounds of submission or the point) to which the notice relates.

(2) A diet ordered under subsection (1) above is in this Act referred to as a "preliminary diet".

(3) The fact that a preliminary diet has been ordered on a particular notice under subsection (1) above shall not preclude the court's consideration at that diet of any other such notice as is mentioned in that subsection, which has been intimated to the court and to the other parties at least 24 hours before that diet.

(4) Subject to subsection (5) below, the court may on ordering a preliminary diet postpone the trial diet for a period not exceeding 21 days; and any such postponement (including postponement for a period which by virtue of the said subsection (5) exceeds 21 days) shall not count towards any time limit applying in respect of the case.

(5) Any period mentioned in subsection (4) above may be extended by the High Court in respect of the case.

(6) Where a preliminary diet is ordered the accused (or all the accused as the case may be) shall attend it; and he (or they as the case may be) shall be required at the conclusion thereof to state how he pleads (or they plead) to the indictment:

Provided that if the court so permits the diet may proceed notwithstanding the absence of an accused.

(7) In subsection (1) above, "appropriate period" means as regards notice—

(*a*) under paragraph (*a*) of that subsection, the period of 15 clear days after service of the indictment;

(*b*) under paragraph (*b*) of that subsection, the period from service of the indictment to 10 clear days before the trial diet; and

(*c*) under paragraph (*c*) of that subsection, the period from service of the indictment to the trial diet.

SCH. 4

Appeal in connection with preliminary diet.

76A.—(1) Without prejudice to any right of appeal under section 228 or 280A of this Act, a party may, with the leave of the court of first instance (granted either on the motion of that party or *ex proprio motu*) and in accordance with such procedure as may be prescribed by Act of Adjournal under this Act, appeal to the High Court against a decision at a preliminary diet; but any such appeal must be taken not later than 2 days after such decision.

(2) Where an appeal is taken under subsection (1) above, the High Court may postpone the trial diet for such period as appears to them to be appropriate and may, if they think fit, direct that such period (or some part of it) shall not count towards any time limit applying in respect of the case.

(3) In disposing of an appeal under subsection (1) above the High Court may affirm the decision of the court of first instance or may remit the case to it with such directions in the matter as they think fit; and where the court of first instance has dismissed the indictment or any part of it, may reverse that decision and direct that the court of first instance fix a trial diet (if it has not already fixed one as regards so much of the indictment as it has not dismissed).".

6. For section 77 (alteration of diet) there shall be substituted the following section—

"Alteration of trial diet

77. Where an indictment is not brought to trial at the trial diet and a warrant for a subsequent sitting of the court, on a day within—

(*a*) in the case of the High Court, two months; or

(*b*) in the case of the sheriff court, one month,

after the date of the aforesaid trial diet has been issued under section 69 of this Act by the clerk of court it shall be lawful for the court to adjourn the trial diet to the subsequent sitting; and the warrant shall have effect as if the trial diet had originally been fixed for the date of the subsequent sitting.".

7. After section 77, there shall be inserted the following section—

"Application for postponement of trial diet.

77A.—(1) At any time before the trial diet, a party may apply to the court before which the trial is to take place for postponement of the trial diet.

(2) Subject to subsection (3) below, after hearing all the parties, the court may discharge the trial diet and either fix a new trial diet or give leave to the prosecutor to serve a notice fixing a new trial diet.

(3) Where all the parties join in an application to postpone the trial diet, the court may proceed under subsection (2) above without hearing the parties.

(4) Where there is a hearing under this section the accused (or all the accused as the case may be) shall attend it:

Provided that if the court so permits the hearing may proceed notwithstanding his (or their) absence.".

8. For section 78 there shall be substituted the following section—

"Record copy of indictment and list of witnesses.

78.—(1) Except in a case to which section 102 of this Act applies, the record copy of the indictment shall on or before the date of service of the indictment be lodged with the clerk of the court before which the trial is to take place; and a copy of the list of witnesses and a copy of the list of productions shall be lodged with him not less than 10 clear days before the trial diet.

(2) The list of productions shall include the record, made under section 20B of this Act (with any rectification, authorised under subsection (4) of that section, incorporated), of proceedings at the examination of the accused.".

9. For section 80 there shall be substituted the following section—

"Objection to witness.

80.—(1) Any objection in respect of misnomer or misdescription of—

(a) any person named in the indictment; or

(b) any witness in the list of witnesses,

shall be intimated in writing to the court before which the trial is to take place, to the prosecutor and to any other accused not less than 10 clear days before the trial diet; and, except on cause shown, no such objection shall be admitted at the trial diet unless so intimated.

(2) Where such intimation has been given or cause is shown and the court is satisfied that the accused making the objection has not been supplied with sufficient information to enable him to identify the person named in the indictment or to find such witness in sufficient time to precognose him before the trial, the court may grant such remedy by postponement, adjournment or otherwise as appears to it to be appropriate.".

10. In section 82(2) and (3) (written notice of witnesses and productions) for the words "second diet" in each of the four places where they occur there shall be substituted the words "trial diet".

11. In section 83 (accused to see productions) for the words "second diet", in both places where they occur, there shall be substituted the words "trial diet".

12. In section 84 (proof as to productions) for the words "second diet", in each of the four places where they occur, there shall be substituted the words "trial diet".

13. In section 96 (notice of jury list) for the words from "Clerk of Justiciary" to "sheriff court", there shall be substituted the words

SCH. 4

" clerk of the court before which the trial is to take place," and for the words " second diet " where they occur for the fourth time, there shall be substituted the words " trial diet ".

14. For section 103, there shall be substituted the following section—

" Pleas of guilty.

103.—(1) Where at any diet the accused tenders a plea of guilty to the indictment or any part thereof he shall be required to sign a written copy of the plea (if he is able to do so); and the judge shall countersign such copy.

(2) Where the plea is to part only of the charge and the prosecutor does not accept such plea, such non-acceptance shall be recorded.

(3) Where a person charged on indictment with any offence tenders a plea of guilty to any other offence of which he could competently be found guilty on the trial of such indictment, and that plea is accepted by the prosecutor, it shall be competent to convict such person of the offence to which he has so pled guilty and to sentence him accordingly.

(4) Nothing in subsection (1) above shall require a plea by or on behalf of a company to be signed.".

15. For section 104 there shall be substituted the following section—

" Remit to High Court for sentence.

104.—(1) Where at any diet in proceedings on indictment in the sheriff court, sentence falls to be imposed but the sheriff holds that any competent sentence which he can impose is inadequate so that the question of sentence is appropriate for the High Court, he shall—

(*a*) endorse upon the record copy of the indictment a certificate of the plea or the verdict (as the case may be);

(*b*) by interlocutor written on such record copy remit the convicted person to the High Court for sentence; and

(*c*) append to such interlocutor a note of his reasons for such remit;

and such remit shall be sufficient warrant to bring the accused before the High Court for sentence and shall remain in force until the convicted person is sentenced.

(2) When the Clerk of Justiciary receives the record copy of the indictment he shall send a copy of the note of reasons to the convicted person or his solicitor and to the Crown Agent.

(3) Subject to subsection (2) above, the note of reasons shall be available only to the High Court and the parties.".

16. Section 105 (High Court case) shall cease to have effect.

SCH. 4

17. Section 106 (pleas of guilty) shall cease to have effect.

18. Section 107 (solicitor of place of second diet may defend at both diets) shall cease to have effect.

19. Section 108 (certain objections competent only at first diet) shall be amended as follows—

(*a*) for the words " unless the same be stated to the sheriff at the first diet before the accused is called upon to plead " there shall be substituted the words " except by leave of the court on cause shown, unless his intention to raise the objection is stated in a notice under section 76(1)(*a*) of this Act ";

(*b*) the words of section 108 as amended by sub-paragraph (*a*) of this paragraph shall be subsection (1) of that section and after that subsection there shall be inserted the following subsection—

" (2) Except by leave of the court on cause shown—

(*a*) no matter relating to the competency or relevancy of the indictment shall be raised ;

(*b*) no plea in bar of trial shall be submitted ; and

(*c*) no application for separation or conjunction of charges or trials shall be submitted,

unless the intention to do so has been stated in a notice under section 76(1) of this Act.".

20. In section 110 (where sentence delayed, original warrant of commitment stands) for the words " the first " there shall be substituted the word " any ".

21. In section 115 (sittings dispensed with) for the words " sheriff at the first ", there shall be substituted the word " trial ".

22. In section 116 (adjournment of second diet)—

(*a*) for the words " the second "—

(i) where they occur for the first time there shall be substituted the words " the trial " ; and

(ii) where they occur for the second time there shall be substituted the words " any further " ; and

(*b*) for the words " at the first diet " there shall be substituted the words " before that diet ".

23. In section 117 (sitting transferred where few cases) for the words " at the first " there shall be substituted the words " before the trial " ; and for the words " the second diets " there shall be substituted the words " any further diets in ".

24. Section 120 (notification after first diet of intention to plead guilty) shall cease to have effect.

25. Section 121 (second diet—transcript of procedure at first diet) shall cease to have effect.

26. Section 122 (review at second diet in High Court) shall cease to have effect.

SCH. 4

27. In section 127(1) (procedure where trial does not take place)—

(*a*) for the words " second diet " in each of the three places where they occur there shall be substituted the words " trial diet " ; and

(*b*) for the words " of the causes set forth in section 122 of this Act," there shall be substituted the word " cause ; ".

Section 45(2).

SCHEDULE 5

YOUNG OFFENDERS

1963 c. 39.

In the Criminal Justice (Scotland) Act 1963—

1. In section 10(3), at the end, there shall be added the following proviso—

" Provided that section 12 of this Act and section 212, or as the case may be 421, of the Criminal Procedure (Scotland) Act 1975 shall continue to apply to a person so transferred to prison.".

2. For section 12 there shall be substituted the following section—

" Supervision of person released from young offenders institution.

12.—(1) This section applies in relation to persons sentenced under section 207 or 415 of the Criminal Procedure (Scotland) Act 1975.

(2) Subject to sections 212 and 421 of the said Act of 1975 (which relate to recall of young offenders on re-conviction) and to subsections (4) to (6) and (9) below, a person in relation to whom this section applies may where he has been sentenced to a period of (or, as the case may be, periods totalling) 6 months or more be required, by notice of the Secretary of State given to the person on his release from that detention, both to be under the supervision of such officer as may be specified in the notice and to comply, while under the supervision, with such conditions as may be so specified ; and the supervision shall continue—

(*a*) in a case where such release is on licence under section 60(1) or section 61 of the Criminal Justice Act 1967, until the expiry of the period of 12 months from the date of such release or until the expiry of the licence, whichever is the later ;

(*b*) in any other case—

(i) where the term was less than 18 months, until the expiry of the period of 6 months from the date of such release ; or

(ii) where the term was 18 months or more, until the expiry of the period of 12 months from the date of such release.

(3) In a case such as is mentioned in paragraph (*a*) of subsection (2) above, the requirement and conditions

specified by the Secretary of State under that subsection shall be in addition to any conditions specified in the licence mentioned in that paragraph. Sch. 5

(4) Without prejudice to subsection (7) below, a period of supervision required under subsection (2) above shall not extend beyond the date on which the person under supervision attains the age of 23 years.

(5) The Secretary of State may by order extend the provisions of subsection (2) above to persons in relation to whom this section applies whose detention is for less than 6 but not less than 3 months.

(6) The Secretary of State may, on giving notice to the person concerned, at any time modify or cancel a requirement, or condition, which is specified under subsection (2) above.

(7) Subject to subsections (8) and (9) below where, before the expiration of the period for which a person is required under this section to be under supervision, the Secretary of State is satisfied that the person has failed to conform to the requirement or has failed to comply with a condition for the time being specified in the notice given to him under subsection (2) above, he may (except in a case such as is mentioned in paragraph (*a*) of subsection (2) above) recall the person to a young offenders institution ; and thereupon the person shall be liable to be detained in that institution for a period not exceeding 3 months, and if at large shall be deemed to be unlawfully at large.

(8) A recall under subsection (7) above shall cease to have effect at the expiration of the first period mentioned in that subsection unless the person to whom it relates is then in custody thereunder.

(9) The Secretary of State may at any time release a person who is, by virtue of subsection (7) above, detained ; and the provisions of this section shall apply to that person as if, following the release mentioned in subsection (2) above, neither the recall under the said subsection (7) nor the subsequent release under this subsection had taken place, except that the period of detention between the recall and the subsequent release shall be deducted from the period for which the person would otherwise be liable to be detained were he again to be recalled.".

3. In section 51(5) (interpretation) for the words from " section 1 " to " of age) " there shall be substituted the words " section 205, 206, 207 or 415 of the Criminal Procedure (Scotland) Act 1975 (restrictions on imprisonment of children etc.) ".

SCHEDULE 6

Section 83(1).

Transitional Provisions

1. A provision contained in any of sections 6, 12 to 17, 26, 28 29, 31, 36, 40 to 42 and 46(1)(*b*) of, and Schedules 1 and 4 to, this

SCH. 6

Act and any related amendment or repeal provided for in Schedule 7 or 8 to this Act, shall not apply in relation to proceedings which have been instituted before the coming into force of that provision; and, for the purposes of this paragraph, proceedings shall be taken to have been instituted on the day on which the petition or complaint is served on the accused.

2. A provision contained in any of sections 18(2), 19, 21, 22, 27, 30 and 39 of this Act, and any such related amendment or repeal, shall not apply in relation to a trial which has commenced before the coming into force of that provision; and, for the purposes of this paragraph, a trial shall be taken to commence—

(*a*) in the case of solemn proceedings, when the oath is administered to the jury;

(*b*) in the case of summary proceedings, when the first witness is sworn.

3. A provision contained in any of sections 47, 48, 50 and 52 of this Act, and any such related amendment or repeal, shall not apply in relation to the enforcement of any fine or caution imposed before the coming into force of that provision.

4. A provision contained in any of sections 46(1)(*a*), (*c*) and (*d*), 56(1) and 57 of this Act shall not affect the punishment for an offence committed before the coming into force of that provision.

5. A person serving a sentence of borstal training on the date when section 45 of this Act comes into force, shall be liable to be detained in a young offenders institution, but in every other respect shall be liable to be dealt with as if the said section had not come into force.

6. Sections 33, 35 and 37 of, and Schedule 2 to, this Act shall not apply in relation to an appeal against, or review of, an order made on the final determination of a solemn prosecution before the coming into force of those sections and that Schedule.

7. Section 34 of, and Schedule 3 to, this Act shall not apply in relation to an appeal against an order made on the final determination of a summary prosecution before the coming into force of that section and Schedule.

8. A provision contained in paragraph 24 of Schedule 7 to this Act shall not affect the operation of the Rehabilitation of Offenders Act 1974 as regards any disposal which predates the coming into force of that provision.

9. In the application of section 66 of this Act to proceedings instituted before the coming into force of the Magistrates' Courts Act 1980, for the reference to section 91 of that Act in subsection (1) of the said section 66 there shall be substituted a reference to section 72B of the Magistrates' Courts Act 1952.

10. In the application of section 38A of the Criminal Law Act 1977 to the execution of extract convictions and warrants before the coming into force of the Magistrates' Courts Act 1980, for the reference to

section 150(3) of the said Act of 1980 in the said section 38A there shall be substituted a reference to section 102(4) of the Magistrates' Courts Act 1952. Sch. 6

SCHEDULE 7

Section 83(2).

Minor and Consequential Amendments

The Prisons (Scotland) Act 1952 (c.61)

1. In section 14 (legalised police cells), after subsection (7), there shall be added the following subsection—

"(8) For the purposes of sections 7 and 35 of this Act, legalised police cells shall be deemed to be prisons.".

2. In section 28(2) (discontinuance of prison) for the words "young offenders institution or Borstal institution" there shall be substituted the words "or young offenders institution".

3. In section 31 (remand centres, etc.)—

(*a*) in subsection (1)—

(i) in paragraph (*b*) for the words from "not less" to "1949" there shall be substituted the words "upon whom detention therein has been imposed under section 207 or 415 of the Criminal Procedure (Scotland) Act 1975";

(ii) paragraph (*c*) shall cease to have effect; and

(iii) in paragraph (*d*) for the words "the Criminal Justice (Scotland) Act 1963" there shall be substituted the words "section 207 or 415 of the Criminal Procedure (Scotland) Act 1975";

(*b*) in subsection (3) ,for the words "young offenders institution and Borstal institution" there shall be substituted the words "and young offenders institution"; and

(*c*) in subsection (4), for the words "young offenders institutions and Borstal institutions" there shall be substituted the words "and young offenders institutions" and for the words "young offenders institutions or Borstal institutions" there shall be substituted the words "or young offenders institutions".

4 In section 34 (temporary detention) for the words "Borstal institution or a young offenders institution" there shall be substituted the words "young offenders institution or a detention centre".

5. In section 35 (rules for the management of prisons and other institutions)—

(*a*) in subsection (1), for the words "young offenders institutions and Borstal institutions" there shall be substituted the words "and young offenders institutions";

(*b*) in subsection (5)(*c*), for the words "Criminal Appeal (Scotland) Act 1926" there shall be substituted the words "Criminal Procedure (Scotland) Act 1975"; and

SCH. 7

(c) in subsection (6), for the words ", corrective training, preventive detention, detention in a young offenders institution or Borstal training" there shall be substituted the words "or detention".

6. In section 37 (persons unlawfully at large)—

(a) in subsection (1), for the words from "corrective training" to "detained in a" there shall be substituted the words "or to detention in a young offenders institution or";

(b) in subsection (2)—

(i) for the words from "corrective training" to "detained in a" there shall be substituted the words "or to detention in a young offenders institution or"; and

(ii) the words "Borstal institution", in both places where they occur, shall cease to have effect; and

(c) after subsection (2) there shall be inserted the following subsection—

"(2A) Without prejudice to section 69(2) of the Criminal Justice Act 1967, in subsection (2) above references to a prison shall be construed as including references to a place which is the subject of a direction of the Secretary of State under section 206(1) of the Criminal Procedure (Scotland) Act 1975.".

The Criminal Justice Act 1961 (*c.* 39)

7. In section 26 (transfer to serve sentence)—

(a) in subsection (5)—

(i) for the words "any part of the United Kingdom other than Northern Ireland" there shall be substituted the words "England and Wales";

(ii) for the words "that part of the United Kingdom" there shall be substituted the words "England and Wales"; and

(iii) the proviso shall cease to have effect;

(b) after subsection (5A) there shall be inserted the following subsection—

"(5B) Where a person sentenced to borstal training is transferred under this section to Scotland the provisions applicable to him shall be those applicable to a person sentenced in Scotland to detention in a young offenders institution:

Provided that—

(a) the maximum and minimum periods for which he may be detained in a young offenders institution shall be those prescribed by section 45(2) of the Prison Act 1952 as amended by section 11 of this Act;

(b) at any time after the expiry of such minimum period he may be released on the direction of the Secretary of State; and

(c) the period after his release (whether on a direction under paragraph (*b*) above or on the expiry of such maximum period) during which he remains under supervision and liable to be recalled shall be that which would have applied under the law of the place where he was sentenced if he had been released there.". Sch. 7

8. In section 29(1) (removal for judicial purposes) after the words " young offenders centre " there shall be inserted the words " , young offenders institution ".

9. In section 30(3) (prisoners unlawfully at large) after the words " young offenders centre " there shall be inserted the words " young offenders institution ".

10. In section 32(2) (extension throughout the United Kingdom of certain enactments relating to supervision and recall)—

(*a*) paragraph (*b*) shall cease to have effect ;

(*b*) in paragraph (*f*), the word " 11 " shall cease to have effect ; and

(*c*) in paragraph (*i*) for the words " 214 " there shall be substituted the words " 212, 214, 421 ".

11. In section 38 (construction of references to sentence of imprisonment)—

(*a*) in subsection (3)(*a*)—

(i) the words " corrective training, preventive detention," shall cease to have effect ;

(ii) at the end there shall be added the words " or young offenders institution " ; and

(*b*) in subsection (5)(*a*), the words " in a young offenders institution " shall cease to have effect.

12. In section 39(1) (interpretation)—

(*a*) in paragraph (*a*) of the definition of " appropriate institution ", for the words " any part of the United Kingdom other than Northern Ireland " there shall be substituted the words " England and Wales " ;

(*b*) in paragraph (*b*) of that definition, the words " England and Wales or " shall cease to have effect ; and

(*c*) in paragraph (*bb*) of that definition, for the words " sentenced to imprisonment when under twenty-one years of age " there shall be substituted the words " under twenty-one years of age who is serving a sentence of—

(i) imprisonment ;

(ii) borstal training ; or

(iii) detention in a young offenders centre in Northern Ireland,

and ".

Sch. 7

The Criminal Justice (Scotland) Act 1963 (*c.* 39)

13. In section 9(4)(*a*) (transfer between institutions), after the words "1957" there shall be inserted the words "the Armed Forces Act 1976".

14. In section 50(2) (general provision as to orders), for the words "12(2)" there shall be substituted the words "12(5)".

15. In section 51 (interpretation)—

(*a*) in subsection (2), for the words "or the Air Force Act 1955" there shall be substituted the words "the Air Force Act 1955 or the Armed Forces Act 1976"; and

(*b*) in subsection (3), for the words "in a young offenders institution" there shall be substituted the words "under section 207 or 415 of the Criminal Procedure (Scotland) Act 1975".

The Legal Aid (Scotland) Act 1967 (*c*.43)

16. In section 1 (scope and general conditions of legal aid), at the end of subsection (7) there shall be added the following proviso—

": Provided that nothing in this section shall preclude a person from being given legal aid in connection with summary proceedings after conviction and before sentence where the court is considering a sentence of imprisonment or detention or the imposition of imprisonment, or detention, under section 396(2) of the Criminal Procedure (Scotland) Act 1975 in respect of failure to pay a fine, and he has not previously been sentenced to imprisonment, or detention as defined in section 41(2)(*b*) of the Criminal Justice (Scotland) Act 1980.".

The Criminal Justice Act 1967 (*c*.80)

17. In section 60(8)(*b*) (release on licence), for the words "in a young offenders institution as defined in section 31(1)(*d*) of the Prisons (Scotland) Act 1952" there shall be substituted the words "under section 207 or 415 of the Criminal Procedure (Scotland) Act 1975".

18. In section 61 (release on licence of persons sentenced to imprisonment for life etc.), in subsection (4) for paragraphs (*a*) and (*b*) there shall be substituted the following paragraphs—

"(*a*) in subsection (1) for the words from 'section' to the end there shall be substituted the words 'section 205(2) or (3) of the Criminal Procedure (Scotland) Act 1975 (persons under 21 convicted of murder); but shall not release on licence such a person except after consultation with the Lord Justice General together with the trial judge if available.';

(*b*) subsection (3) shall be omitted.".

19. In section 62 (revocation of licences, etc.)—

(*a*) in subsection (11), for the words "206" there shall be substituted the words "205(2)"; and (*b*) after subsection (11) there shall be added the following subsection— Sch. 7

"(12) This section shall have effect, in its application to a person sentenced to be detained under section 205(3), 207 or 415 of the said Act of 1975 (detention of young offenders) as if for any reference to a prison there were substituted a reference to a young offenders institution.".

20. In section 64(2)(*a*) (conditions in licences of persons transferred from another part of the United Kingdom, the Channel Islands or the Isle of Man), for the words "section 60" there shall be substituted the words "sections 60 and 61".

The Social Work (Scotland) Act 1968 (*c*.49)

21. In section 42 (conduct of children's hearing and application to sheriff for findings), after subsection (2) there shall be inserted the following subsection—

"(2A) Where the ground for referral is that the child is in need of compulsory measures of care because he has committed an offence, the sheriff to whom an application under subsection (2)(*c*) above shall be made shall be the sheriff who would have jurisdiction if the child were being prosecuted for that offence.".

The Road Traffic Act 1972 (*c*.20)

22. In section 10(4) (evidence by certificate)—

(*a*) after the word "Scotland" there shall be inserted "—(*a*)"; and

(*b*) at the end there shall be inserted the following paragraph—

"(*b*) A written execution purporting to be signed by the person who served a copy of the certificate or of the notice in terms of subsection (3) above, together with, where appropriate, a post office receipt for the relative registered or recorded delivery letter shall be sufficient evidence of service of such a copy.".

23. In section 94(3), for the word "conviction" there shall be substituted the word "sentence".

The Rehabilitation of Offenders Act 1974 (*c*. 53)

24. In section 5 (rehabilitation periods for particular sentences)—

(*a*) in subsection (1)(*d*)—

(i) after the word "life", there shall be inserted the words "or under section 205(2) or (3) of the Criminal Procedure (Scotland) Act 1975,"; and

(ii) for the words "or under section 57 of the Children and Young Persons (Scotland) Act 1937 (young offenders convicted of grave crimes)" there shall be substituted the words "(young offenders convicted of grave crimes) or under section 206 of the said Act of 1975 (detention of children convicted on indictment)";

(*b*) in subsection (2), in Table B, in the first column—

(i) for the words "57 of the said Act of 1937" there shall be substituted the words "206 of the Criminal Procedure (Scotland) Act 1975"; and

SCH. 7

(ii) the words " or under section 7 of the Criminal Justice (Scotland) Act 1963 " shall cease to have effect ;

(*c*) in subsection (5) for paragraph (*c*) there shall be substituted the following paragraph—

" (*c*) an order under section 413 of the Criminal Procedure (Scotland) Act 1975 committing a child for the purpose of his undergoing residential training ; " ; and

(*d*) in subsection (9)—

(i) in paragraph (*a*), for the words " in a young offenders institution in Scotland " there shall be substituted the words " under section 207 or 415 of the Criminal Procedure (Scotland) Act 1975 " ; and

(ii) in paragraph (*b*) for the words " section 57 of the said Act of 1937 " there shall be substituted the words " section 206 of the said Act of 1975 ".

The Criminal Procedure (Scotland) Act 1975 (*c*.21)

25. In section 19(1) (prisoners before examination to have access to solicitor), the existing words after " arrest " shall be paragraph (*a*) of the subsection and after that paragraph there shall be inserted the following paragraph—

" (*b*) to be told what rights there are under paragraph (*a*) above and subsections (2) and (3) below.".

26. At the end of section 28 (admission or refusal of bail after committal), there shall be added the following subsection—

" (3) For the avoidance of doubt, the provisions of section 26 of this Act and the foregoing provisions of this section apply whether or not the person is in custody at such time as he appears for the disposal of his application.".

27. In section 71 (manner of service of indictment, etc.), for the words from " macer " to the end there shall be substituted the words " officer of law ".

28. In section 81 (examination by prosecutor of witnesses not included in lists lodged), at the beginning there shall be inserted the words " Without prejudice to section 82A of this Act,".

29. In section 98 (jurors to be cited by registered letter or recorded delivery), after the word " delivery " there shall be inserted the words " or to be served on him by an officer of law ".

30. In section 100(2) (rules of court in relation to jurors) for the words from " The rules of court " to " to this Act." there shall be substituted the words " The provisions of Schedule 3 to this Act shall have effect as if they were rules of court made under this subsection.".

31. After section 111 there shall be inserted the following section—

" Computation of period.

111A. Where the last day of any period mentioned in section 75, 76, 76A or 80 of this Act falls on a Saturday, Sunday or court holiday, such period shall extend to and include the next day which is not a Saturday, Sunday or court holiday.".

32. In the proviso to section 113(4) (judges in High Court), after the word " importance " there shall be inserted the words " in Edinburgh or on circuit " and after the word " preside " there shall be inserted the words " for the whole or any part of the trial.". Sch. 7

33. In section 141(1) (accused and spouse competent witnesses for defence), for the words " competent witnesses " there shall be substituted the words " a competent witness ".

34. In section 168 (power of court, in respect of certain offences against a child, to refer child to reporter), for the words from " committed " to " reporter " there shall be substituted the words—

" committed any offence—

(*a*) under section 21 of the Children and Young Persons (Scotland) Act 1937 ;

(*b*) mentioned in Schedule 1 to this Act ; or

(*c*) in respect of a female person aged 17 years or over which constitutes the crime of incest,

may refer—

(i) the child in respect of whom the offence mentioned in paragraph (*a*) or (*b*) above has been committed ; or

(ii) any child who is, or who is likely to become, a member of the same household as the person who has committed the offence mentioned in paragraph (*b*) or (*c*) above,

to the reporter ".

35. In section 173(3) (reference and remit of children's cases by courts to children's hearings), for the words " shall request " there shall be substituted the words—

" dealing with the case if it is—

(*a*) the High Court, may ; and

(*b*) the sheriff court, shall,

request ".

36. In section 179 (power of court, in solemn proceedings, to adjourn a case before sentence)—

(*a*) in subsection (1) there shall be inserted before the proviso the words " or ordain him to appear at the adjourned diet " ; and

(*b*) in subsection (2), for paragraph (*a*) there shall be substituted the following paragraph—

" (*a*) review the order appealed against and either grant bail on such conditions as it thinks fit or ordain the accused to appear at the adjourned diet ; ".

37. In section 193A (fines on conviction on indictment to be without limit), after the word " summarily " there shall be inserted the words—

" other than by virtue of section 8 of the Criminal Justice (Scotland) Act 1980 ".

SCH. 7

38. In section 212 (recall to young offenders institution on reconviction), in subsection (1)—

(i) for the words " young offenders institution " there shall be substituted the words " under section 207 of this Act " ; and

(ii) for the words from " instead " to the end there shall be substituted the words ", except where the person convicted is subject to a licence granted under section 60 (1) or section 61 of the Criminal Justice Act 1967, make an order for his recall.".

39. For section 215 (legal custody) there shall be substituted the following section—

" Legal custody. 215. Any person required or authorised by or under this Act or Part I of the Criminal Justice (Scotland) Act 1980 to be taken to any place, or to be detained or kept in custody shall, while being so taken or detained or kept, be deemed to be in legal custody.".

40. In section 218 (consideration of time spent in custody), the words " in a young offenders institution as defined in section 31(1)(*d*) of the Prisons (Scotland) Act 1952 " shall cease to have effect.

41. In section 241 (notice to authorities, etc. of date of hearing), for the words " Prison Commissioners for Scotland " in both places where they occur there shall be substituted the words " Secretary of State ".

42. In section 242 (notice to Prison Commissioners of attendance of appellant at hearing), for the words " Prison Commissioners for Scotland " and " said Commissioners " there shall in each case be substituted the words " Secretary of State ".

43. In section 243 (warders to attend court), for the words " Prison Commissioners for Scotland " there shall be substituted the words " Secretary of State " and for the word " warders " there shall be substituted the words " prison officers ".

44. In section 251(5) (appeal against refusal of application), for the words " Prison Commissioners for Scotland " there shall be substituted the words " Secretary of State ".

45. In section 261 (notice of determination of appeal), for the words " Prison Commissioners for Scotland " there shall be substituted the words " Secretary of State ".

46. In section 268(4) (reckoning of time spent pending appeal) for the words " Borstal institution " there shall be substituted the words " young offenders institution ".

47. In section 282 (Acts of Adjournal), the existing words shall be subsection (1) and at the end of that subsection there shall be added the following subsection—

"(2) The High Court may by Act of Adjournal modify, amend or repeal any enactment, including an enactment contained in this Part of this Act, in so far as that enactment relates to matters with respect to which an Act of Adjournal may be made under subsection (1) above.". SCH. 7

48. In section 283(1) (application of Part II of this Act)—

(*a*) in paragraph (*b*) for the word " statute " there shall be substituted the words " enactment or rule of law " ; and

(*b*) at the end of that paragraph there shall be inserted the words " as well as, in accordance with section 196(1) of this Act, to the enforcement of a fine imposed in solemn proceedings ".

49. In section 283A(1) (offences which are to become triable only summarily), at the beginning there shall be inserted the words—

" Subject to section 8 of the Criminal Justice (Scotland) Act 1980, but otherwise ".

50. In section 289D (power to alter sums specified in certain provisions)—

(*a*) in subsection (2), after the word " (3) " there shall be inserted the words " or (3A) " ; and

(*b*) after subsection (3) there shall be inserted the following subsection—

" (3A) This subsection applies to a sum mentioned in—

(*a*) section 186(2)(*a*) of this Act in relation to the penalty for a breach of a probation order ;

(*b*) section 284(*b*) of this Act in relation to the power of the district court to impose a fine on conviction of a common law offence ;

(*c*) section 284(*c*) of this Act in relation to the power of the district court to ordain the accused to find caution on conviction of a common law offence ;

(*d*) section 285(*b*)(iii) of this Act in relation to the jurisdiction of the district court to try certain common law offences ;

(*e*) section 312(*z*) of this Act in relation to stating the value of property in a charge ;

(*f*) section 344(1) of this Act in relation to the penalty for certain contempts of court ;

(*g*) section 387(2)(*a*) of this Act in relation to the penalty for breach of a probation order ;

(*h*) section 407(1A) of this Act in relation to imprisonment for non-payment of a fine or for failure to find caution ;

(*i*) section 435(*e*) of this Act in relation to the award of expenses against an accused ;

(*j*) section 453(3) of this Act in relation to the award of expenses to an appellant ;

(*k*) section 7(1) of the Criminal Justice (Scotland) Act 1980 in relation to the jurisdiction of the district court to try certain statutory offences ;

Sch. 7

(*l*) section 9(2) of the said Act of 1980 in relation to the penalty for failure to attend for precognition on oath;

(*m*) section 9(3) of the said Act of 1980 in relation to the penalty for refusal to give evidence, or for prevarication, during precognition on oath; or

(*n*) section 59(3)(*b*) of the said Act of 1980 in relation to the power of the district court to make a compensation order.".

51. At the end of section 298 (all offences to be bailable), there shall be added the following subsection—

"(3) For the avoidance of doubt, the foregoing provisions of this section apply whether or not the person is in custody at such time as he appears for the disposal of his application.".

52. In section 305 (intimation to solicitor)—

(*a*) for the word "apprehended" and for the word "apprehension" there shall be substituted respectively the word "arrested" and the words "such arrest";

(*b*) the existing words after "entitled" shall be paragraph (*a*) of the section; and

(*c*) after that paragraph there shall be inserted the following paragraph—

"(*b*) to be told what his rights under paragraph (*a*) above are.".

53. In section 310 (incidental applications), after the words "prior to" there shall be inserted the words "or after"; and the word "subsequent" where it first occurs shall cease to have effect.

54. In section 334 (procedure at first diet, etc.)—

(*a*) in subsection (1) for the words from "objections" where it first occurs to "stated" there shall be substituted the words "an objection to the competency or relevancy of the complaint or the proceedings or issue a denial that he is the person charged by the police with the offence; and no such objection or denial shall be allowed to be stated or issued";

(*b*) for subsection (2) there shall be substituted the following subsection—

"(2) In the absence of the accused, an objection to the competency or relevancy of a summary complaint or the proceedings thereon may be stated, or a denial that the accused is the person charged by the police with the offence may be issued, by counsel or by a solicitor on his behalf; and where such an objection is stated or denial is issued, the provisions of this Part of this Act shall apply in like manner as if the accused had appeared and stated the objection or issued the denial.".

55. In section 344(4)(*a*) (failure of witness to attend for precognition) for the words "24" there shall be substituted the words "48".

56. In section 346(1) (accused and spouse competent witnesses for defence), for the words "competent witnesses" there shall be substituted the words "a competent witness".

57. In section 364 (power of court, in respect of certain offences against a child, to refer child to reporter), for the words from "committed" to "reporter" there shall be substituted the words—

"committed any offence—

(*a*) under section 21 of the Children and Young Persons (Scotland) Act 1937;

(*b*) mentioned in Schedule 1 to this Act; or

(*c*) in respect of a female person aged 17 years or over which constitutes the crime of incest,

may refer—

(i) the child in respect of whom the offence referred to in paragraph (*a*) or (*b*) above has been committed; or

(ii) any child who is, or who is likely to become, a member of the same household as the person who has committed the offence mentioned in paragraph (*b*) or (*c*) above,

to the reporter".

58. In section 370 (child charged jointly with person who is not a child) for the words ", 367 and 374" there shall be substituted the words "and 367".

59. In section 380 (power of court, in summary proceedings, to adjourn a case before sentence)—

(*a*) in subsection (1) there shall be inserted before the proviso the words "or ordain him to appear at the adjourned diet"; and

(*b*) in subsection (2), for paragraph (*a*) there shall be substituted the following paragraph—

"(*a*) review the order appealed against and either grant bail on such conditions as it thinks fit or ordain the accused to appear at the adjourned diet;".

60. In section 395(2) (provisions as to fines), for the words "detention centre" there shall be substituted the words "young offenders institution".

61. In section 398(1) (restriction on imprisonment after fine or caution), for the words "his means in his presence" there shall be substituted the words "in his presence the reason why the fine has not been paid".

62. In section 399 (payment of fine by instalments)—

(*a*) in subsection (1), the words from "and it" to the end shall cease to have effect; and

(*b*) for subsection (2) there shall be substituted the following subsections—

"(2) Where the court has ordered payment of a fine by instalments it may—

(a) allow further time for payment of any instalment thereof;

SCH. 7

(*b*) order payment thereof by instalments of lesser amounts, or at longer intervals, than those originally fixed.

(3) The powers conferred by subsection (2) above shall be exercisable without requiring the attendance of the accused.".

63. At the end of section 401 (supplementary provisions as to payment of fine) there shall be added the following subsection—

"(3) Where a warrant has been issued for the apprehension of an offender for non-payment of a fine, the offender may, notwithstanding section 412 of this Act, pay such fine in full to a constable ; and the warrant shall not then be enforced and the constable shall remit the fine to the clerk of court.".

64. In section 407(3) (period of imprisonment for non-payment of fine) for the words "subsection (1)" there shall be substituted the words "subsection (1A)".

65. In section 409(1) (payment of fine in part by prisoner), for the words from "by a number" to the end there shall be substituted the words "(or as the case may be further reduced) by a number of days bearing as nearly as possible the same proportion to such term as the sum so paid bears to the amount of the fine outstanding at the commencement of the imprisonment:

Provided that the day on which any sum is paid shall not be regarded as a day served by the prisoner as part of the said term of imprisonment.".

66. In section 411(1) (recovery by civil diligence), for the words "poinding the sale", "ten free" and "small debt court" there shall be substituted, respectively, the words "poinding and sale", "14" and "in a summary cause".

67. In section 421(1) (recall to young offenders institution on reconviction)—

(*a*) for the words "young offenders institution" there shall be substituted the words "under section 415 of this Act"; and

(*b*) for the words from "instead" to the end there shall be substituted the words ", except where the person convicted is subject to a licence granted under section 60(1) or section 61 of the Criminal Justice Act 1967, make an order for his recall.".

68. In section 424 (detention in precincts of court), after the word "imprisonment" there shall be inserted the words "or detention".

69. For section 426 (legal custody) there shall be substituted the following section—

"Legal custody.

426. Any person required or authorised by or under this Act or Part I of the Criminal Justice (Scotland) Act 1980 to be taken to any place, or to be detained or kept in custody shall, while being so taken or detained or kept, be deemed to be in legal custody.".

70. In section 431 (consideration of time spent in custody), the words " in a young offenders institution as defined in section 31(1)(*d*) of the Prisons (Scotland) Act 1952 " shall cease to have effect. SCH. 7

71. For section 436 (forfeiture of implements) there shall be substituted the same provisions as constitute section 223 (forfeiture of property).

72. In section 457 (Acts of Adjournal), at the end there shall be added the following paragraph—

" (*d*) to modify, amend or repeal any enactment, including an enactment contained in this Part of this Act, in so far as that enactment relates to matters with respect to which an Act of Adjournal may be made under this section.".

73. In section 458 (construction of enactments referring to sentence of detention) for the words " in a young offenders institution " there shall be substituted the words " under section 207 or 415 of this Act ".

74. In section 459 (construction of enactments referring to detention) for the words " in a young offenders institution " there shall be substituted the words " under section 207 or 415 of this Act ".

75. In section 460 (transitional provisions and savings) subsection (6), which is superseded by the provisions inserted by paragraphs 47 and 72 above, shall cease to have effect.

76. In section 462(1) (interpretation)—

(*a*) at the appropriate place there shall be inserted the definition " ' diet ' includes any continuation of a diet ; " ;

(*b*) in the definition of " impose detention " and " impose imprisonment ", for the words " failing to do or abstain from doing anything required to be done or left undone " there shall be substituted the words " contempt of court " ; and

(*c*) for the definition of " sentence " there shall be substituted the definition " ' sentence ', whether of detention or of imprisonment, means a sentence passed in respect of a crime or offence and does not include an order for committal in default of payment of any sum of money or for contempt of court.".

77. In section 463 (extent) after subsection (1) there shall be added the following subsection—

" (1A) Sections 169 and 374 of this Act shall extend to Northern Ireland.".

78. In Schedule 3 (composition of juries)—

(*a*) in paragraph 2—

(i) for the words from " be made " to " by him)." there shall be substituted the words " be lodged, at least 15 clear days before the trial diet, with the clerk of the court before which that diet is to be." ; and

(ii) for the words " the presiding sheriff " there shall be substituted the words " a judge of that court ; and that judge shall deal with the application in chambers. The

SCH. 7

accused, if represented by counsel or by a solicitor, shall not be entitled to attend."; and

(*b*) for paragraphs 3 and 4 there shall be substituted the following paragraph—

"3. The judge's decision under the foregoing rule shall be recorded on the record copy of the indictment and shall be final.".

The Criminal Law Act 1977 (*c.* 45)

79. In section 39(3) (service of summonses and citations throughout the United Kingdom)—

(*a*) after the word "include" there shall be inserted "(*a*)"; and

(*b*) at the end there shall be added the following paragraph—

"(*b*) persons authorised by a chief officer of police in England or Wales to serve summonses there.".

Section 83(3).

SCHEDULE 8

REPEALS

Chapter	Short title	Extent of repeal
7 Anne c. 21.	The Treason Act 1708.	Section 7.
39 & 40 Geo. 3. c. 93.	The Treason Act 1800.	The whole Act.
8 & 9 Vict. c. 33.	The Railways Clauses Consolidation (Scotland) Act 1845.	Section 144.
38 & 39 Vict. c. 86.	The Conspiracy, and Protection of Property Act 1875.	Section 11.
50 & 51 Vict. c. 35.	The Criminal Procedure (Scotland) Act 1887.	Schedules F and G.
55 & 56 Vict. c. 55.	The Burgh Police (Scotland) Act 1892.	Section 382.
2 & 3 Geo. 5. c. 14.	The Protection of Animals (Scotland) Act 1912.	Section 4.
23 & 24 Geo. 5. c. 12.	The Children and Young Persons Act 1933.	Section 26(5).
8 & 9 Geo. 6. c. 44.	The Treason Act 1945.	The whole Act.
12, 13 & 14 Geo. 6. c. 94.	The Criminal Justice (Scotland) Act 1949.	Section 21. Section 75(3)(*e*).
15 & 16 Geo. 6. & 1 Eliz. 2. c. 61.	The Prisons (Scotland) Act 1952.	Section 7(4). Section 19. In section 31(4), in paragraph (i) of the proviso, the words ", section nineteen, subsections (2) to (6) of section twenty"; and paragraph (iv) of the proviso. Sections 32 and 33. Section 35(5)(*a*). In section 37(2), the words "Borstal institution" in both places where they occur.

Sch. 8

Chapter	Short title	Extent of repeal
8 & 9 Eliz. 2. c. 16.	The Road Traffic Act 1960.	Section 246.
9 & 10 Eliz. 2. c. 39.	The Criminal Justice Act 1961.	In section 26(5), in each of paragraphs (*a*) and (*b*) of the proviso, the words " Scotland or ". In section 32(2), paragraph (*b*), and in paragraph (*f*) the word " 11 ". In section 38, in subsection (3)(*a*) the words " corrective training, preventive detention," ; and in subsection (5)(*a*) the words " in a young offenders institution ". In section 39(1), in paragraph (*b*) of the definition of " appropriate institution ", the words " England and Wales or ".
1962 c. 52.	The Penalties for Drunkenness Act 1962.	In section 1(2)(*a*) the words " the first paragraph of subsection (1) of section seventy of the Licensing (Scotland) Act 1903," and in section 1(2)(*b*) the words " or the said section seventy ".
1963 c. 39.	The Criminal Justice (Scotland) Act 1963.	Section 2. Sections 4 and 5. Section 9(1) and (2). Section 11. In section 50(1), the words " (other than orders made under section 11, section 12(1) or (3) or section 22) ".
1967 c. 76.	The Road Traffic Regulation Act 1967.	Section 93.
1967 c. 80.	The Criminal Justice Act 1967.	In section 60— in subsection (6) the words from " —(*a*) " to " case," in paragraph (*b*); and in subsection (8), in paragraph (*c*) the letter " (*a*) ". In section 70(1) the words " corrective training or preventive detention ".
1968 c. 27.	The Firearms Act 1968.	In Schedule 6 Part II, paragraph 1.
1971 c. 77.	The Immigration Act 1971.	In section 6(5) the words " (*a*) except in Scotland " ; and the words from " ; and (*b*) " to the end.
1972 c. 20.	The Road Traffic Act 1972.	In Schedule 4 Part IV, paragraph 3.
1974 c. 53.	The Rehabilitation of Offenders Act 1974.	In section 5(2), in Table B the words " or under section 7 of the Criminal Justice (Scotland) Act 1963 ".

SCH. 8

Chapter	Short title	Extent of repeal
1975 c. 14.	The Social Security Act 1975.	Section 147(6).
1975 c. 21.	The Criminal Procedure (Scotland) Act 1975.	In section 68(3) the words " where the accused pleads not guilty at the first diet ". Section 74(3). Sections 105 to 107. Sections 120 to 122. In section 141, the words " and the spouse of the accused "; in proviso (*b*) the words " or the spouse of the accused "; provisos (*c*) and (*d*); and in proviso (*g*) the words " or section 143 of this Act ". In section 191(1) the words " under this Part of this Act ". In section 193(2) the words from " as " to the end. Section 195. Sections 197 to 202. Section 204. Sections 208 to 211. In section 218 the words " in a young offenders institution as defined in section 31(1)(*d*) of the Prisons (Scotland) Act 1952 ". In section 228, the proviso. Section 229. Section 232. In section 234 in each of subsections (1) and (3) the words " or an applicant for leave to appeal " and the words " or application for leave to appeal ". In section 236 the words " or application for leave to appeal ". In section 240 the words " and on an application for leave to appeal ". In section 245(3) the words " from the sheriff court ". In section 247 the words " to give leave to appeal " and the words " or of an application for leave to appeal ". Section 253(2). In section 257 the words " or applicant " and in both places where they occur the words " or application for leave to appeal ". In section 263(1) the words " or an application for leave to appeal ".

Chapter	Short title	Extent of repeal
1975 c. 21.—*cont.*	The Criminal Procedure (Scotland) Act 1975.—*cont.*	In section 265(3) the words " either upon grounds of law alone, or with the certificate of the said judge upon any grounds mentioned in section 228(*b*) of this Act ". In section 272 the words " or of application for leave to appeal "; in the three places where they occur the words " or application for leave to appeal,"; and the words " or application " in the fourth place where they occur. In section 274(1) the words " or may be authorised " and the words " or application for leave to appeal ". In section 277 the words " and application for leave to appeal "; the words " or application " in both places where they occur; the words " section 229 "; the words " section 232 "; and the words " section 233 ". In section 285, in paragraph (*b*), sub-paragraph (iv), and the proviso. Section 289D(3)(*c*). In section 296(5) the words " (including any continuation of diet) ". In section 310 the word " subsequent " where it first occurs. In section 314(3) the words " or a later ". Section 337(*e*). In section 346, the words " and the spouse of the accused "; in paragraph (*b*) of the proviso the words " or the spouse of the accused "; paragraphs (*c*) and (*d*) of the proviso; and in paragraph (*g*) of the proviso the words " or section 348 of this Act ". Section 365. In section 392(1) the words " on indictment " and the words " under Part I of this Act ". In section 399(1), the words from " and it " to the end. Section 405. Section 410. Section 411(2).

SCH. 8

Chapter	Short title	Extent of repeal
1975 c. 21.—*cont.*	The Criminal Procedure (Scotland) Act 1975.—*cont.*	Section 414. Sections 416 to 420. In section 434(3) the words from " and, without " to the end. Section 444(6). Section 445. In section 447(2) the words from " of the form " to " or ". Section 448(9). Section 454(2). Section 460(5) and (6). Schedule 4. In Schedule 7B, in paragraph 1, sub-paragraphs (1)(*a*) and (2)(*c*). In Schedule 9, paragraph 40.
1975 c. 61.	The Child Benefit Act 1975.	Section 11(8).
1976 c. 66.	The Licensing (Scotland) Act 1976.	Section 128(2).
1976 c. 67.	The Sexual Offences (Scotland) Act 1976.	Section 7. Section 16.
1976 c. 71.	The Supplementary Benefits Act 1976.	Section 26(5).
1977 c. 45.	The Criminal Law Act 1977.	In Schedule 11, paragraphs 11 to 13.
1979 c. 2.	The Customs and Excise Management Act 1979.	Section 149(2).

PRINTED IN ENGLAND BY BERNARD M. THIMONT
Controller of Her Majesty's Stationery Office and Queen's Printer of Acts of Parliament